For my friend C[...]
thanks for everything!

Ted

The Politics of Automobile Insurance Reform

American Governance and Public Policy

A SERIES EDITED BY

Barry Rabe

This series examines a broad range of public policy issues and their relationship to all levels of government in the United States. The editors welcome serious scholarly studies and seek to publish books that appeal to both academic and professional audiences. The series showcases studies that illuminate the successes, as well as the problems, of policy formulation and implementation.

The Politics of Automobile Insurance Reform

Ideas, Institutions, and Public Policy in North America

Edward L. Lascher, Jr.

GEORGETOWN UNIVERSITY PRESS / WASHINGTON, D.C.

Georgetown University Press, Washington, D.C. 20007
© 1999 by Georgetown University Press. All rights reserved.

10 9 8 7 6 5 4 3 2 1   1999

THIS VOLUME IS PRINTED ON ACID-FREE ∞ OFFSET BOOK PAPER

Library of Congress Cataloging-in-Publication Data

Lascher, Edward L.
   The politics of automobile insurance reform : ideas, institutions, and public policy in North America / Edward L. Lascher, Jr.
     p.   cm. — (American governance and public policy)
   Includes bibliographical references and index.
   ISBN 0-87840-739-1
   1. Insurance, Automobile—Government policy—United States.
2. Insurance, Automobile—Government policy—Canada.   I. Title.
II. Series.
HG9970.3.L37   1999
368'.092'097—dc21   99-18215
                                                                                     CIP

For Liz, with love

Contents

Acknowledgments xi

1 Introduction: Why We Should Care about the Politics of Automobile Insurance Reform 1
THE ISSUE FOCUS: AUTOMOBILE INSURANCE REFORM 3,
THE INSTITUTIONAL FOCUS: SEPARATION OF POWERS VERSUS
WESTMINSTER SYSTEM 7,   DATA SUMMARY 9,   ORGANIZATION OF
THE BOOK 9,   NOTES 10

2 Explaining Policy Choices: Pressure versus Ideas 12
PRESSURE THEORY 13,   THE POLITICS OF IDEAS 17,   ASSESSING THE
INFLUENCE OF PRESSURE AND IDEAS ON AUTOMOBILE INSURANCE
REFORM 21,   CONCLUSION 22,   NOTES 23

3 The Profiteering Story and the Pogo Story 24
AN OVERVIEW OF AUTOMOBILE INSURANCE SYSTEMS 25,   WHAT WAS
THE PROBLEM? 28,   POLICY OPTIONS 34,   INTEREST GROUP
POSITIONS 38,   TWO KEY STORIES 40,   SUMMARY OF POLICY
CHANGES 48,   CONCLUSION 49,   NOTES 49

4 Reform Enacted: Pennsylvania 52
CONTEXT 53,   THE BATTLE OVER INSURANCE REFORM 55,
EXPLAINING LEGISLATIVE DECISIONS IN PENNSYLVANIA 62,
EPILOGUE: DID ACT 6 WORK? 65,   NOTES 71

5 Reform Stymied: Rhode Island 74
CONTEXT 75,   THE BATTLE OVER INSURANCE REFORM 76,
EXPLAINING LEGISLATIVE DECISIONS: RHODE ISLAND VERSUS
PENNSYLVANIA 81,   CONCLUSION 87,   NOTES 88

Contents

6 Different Reform Regimes: Ontario 90
CONTEXT FOR THE 1989–1990 NO-FAULT BILL 92, THE BATTLE OVER NO-FAULT INSURANCE 96, EXPLAINING THE ENACTMENT OF NO-FAULT LEGISLATION 99, EPILOGUE: THE NDP AND PUBLIC AUTOMOBILE INSURANCE 102, NOTES 104

7 The Parliamentary System Difference 106
LOSS IMPOSITION AND GOVERNMENTAL SYSTEM DIFFERENCES 106, THE STATES AND THE PROVINCES: AGGREGATE ANALYSIS 108, MINI-CASE STUDIES: MANITOBA, SASKATCHEWAN, AND HAWAII 111, ALTERNATIVE EXPLANATIONS 115, NOTES 117

8 Conclusion: Learning from Automobile Insurance Reform 120
BEYOND AUTOMOBILE INSURANCE REFORM 122, CONCLUSION 124, NOTES 125

Appendix: Notes on Data Sources 127
AGGREGATE DATA 127, SURVEYS 128, CASE STUDIES 128

References 131

Index 139

Acknowledgments

I owe a great deal to three colleagues and friends: Ross Cheit, Mike Powers, and Paul Quirk. Ross and Mike taught me much of what I know about the substance and politics of automobile insurance reform. I learned much of what I know about the politics of ideas from Paul.

Numerous practitioners assisted me in my research by granting me interviews, answering my questions, completing my survey forms, providing me with written materials, etc. With three exceptions, I will refrain from identifying any of them in particular. This is not because my gratitude is small—the opposite is the case. Instead, a) I would be concerned about missing some people if I even tried to make a comprehensive list of all those who were of assistance, and b) some people either requested or would be well served by anonymity.

The three exceptions are Jim Langevin, Sheldon Whitehouse, and former Pennsylvania governor Robert Casey. Jim, a former student who moved on to become Rhode Island's secretary of state, first got me interested in studying decision making in the Ocean State. His assistance in providing the "lay of the land" was very valuable. As director of Rhode Island's Department of Business Regulation, and even after he had moved to become the United States attorney for that state, Sheldon greatly assisted me in understanding events in Rhode Island as well as the nature of the automobile insurance reform controversy. Governor Casey generously granted me an extensive, helpful interview during his last months in office.

Matt Newman provided superb research assistance and wrote the first draft of what would become a "mini–case study" of the automobile insurance reform battle in Hawaii.

My colleagues at the California State University, Sacramento (CSUS) Graduate Program in Public Policy and Administration/Center for California Studies have provided me with a remarkably high-energy, supportive, good-humored, and intellectually challenging environment. I am most grateful to Suzi Byrd, Tim Hodson, Donna Hoenig-Couch, Nancy Shulock, Rob Wassmer, and Bob Waste. I especially wish to thank Cristy Jensen for the continual support and encouragement she has provided ever since I first expressed my interest in coming to CSUS.

For trying out ideas such as those I present in this book, anybody would be lucky to have the kind of sharp, funny, unpretentious students that are in our graduate program. I consider myself very fortunate.

Barry Rabe, the series editor with whom I have been in contact, and John Samples, my editor at Georgetown University Press, have been helpful and professional. My association with them is a source of pride.

An earlier version of the argument presented in chapter 7 appeared in the *Canadian Journal of Political Science* and is cited in full in my references. I am pleased to have an opportunity to use and further the arguments made in that article.

Throughout the (interminable?) process that led to the book you see before you, I was bolstered by continuing encouragement from my mother, stepfather, brother, sister, and brother-in-law. I am sure they helped more than they realized.

Finally, but most importantly, I wish to offer my deepest thanks to Liz, Alex, and Avery for being themselves. And that's pretty wonderful.

Edward L. Lascher, Jr.
Sacramento, California

Auth © The Philadelphia Inquirer. Reprinted with permission of Universal Press Syndicate. All rights reserved.

1
Introduction: Why We Should Care about the Politics of Automobile Insurance Reform

> Political scientists are accustomed to such concepts as power, influence, pressure, and strategy. If we try to understand public policy solely in terms of these concepts, however, we miss a great deal. The content of the ideas themselves, far from being mere smokescreens or rationalizations, are integral parts of decision making in and around government.
>
> —John W. Kingdon (1995, 125)

Why do policymakers choose one approach for tackling a public policy problem and not another? Why do policymakers in different jurisdictions adopt varying alternatives? Why do approaches deviate over time? In answering questions such as these, the scholarly literature—and for that matter, much of the popular literature—has tended to emphasize political pressure. That is, a state adopts policy X (e.g., a managed care approach to controlling health care costs) and not policy Y (e.g., a "single payer" insurance system) because of pressure from interest groups, constituents, etc. Two cities enact different policies because specific interest groups (public employee unions, for example) are stronger in one city than the other. Policy changes in a community after a new group is formed and puts pressure on lawmakers.

Against the view that pressure sufficiently explains differing policy choices, a smaller but growing body of work emphasizes ideas and information.[1] Decision makers not only react to pressures brought to bear on them by groups but act on the basis of their mental conceptions of the merits of policy choices. Policy deliberation shapes which route politicians choose to take. Consequently, if we truly want to understand why, say, one government chooses the managed care option while another adopts the single payer approach, we need to know about what decision makers were thinking about the health care problem, and what kind of information they processed.

This book falls in the latter camp. The core of my argument is that even in some areas that feature vigorous interest group politics, decisions are in large measure determined by how policymakers evaluate likely policy outcomes. In everyday language, policymakers judge any specific policy option in terms of this question: "Will it work?" Variance in responses to this question leads to different decisions.

Yet while this book can be placed within the expanding "politics of ideas" literature, my hope is that it significantly extends what we know about how such ideas work in practice. In particular, I stress a mechanism that has been given insufficient attention to this point: the extent to which policymakers accept causal stories that come to be told in an issue arena. These stories provide means of linking problem diagnosis with possible solutions. The stories also enable politicians (and others) to make sense of numerous but disparate pieces of information.

Are there any practical consequences to failing to appreciate how politicians think about policy effectiveness? My contention is that there are. That is, we risk both misinterpreting past events and making unwarranted predictions about the future course of public policy. To be more concrete, pressure theory models predict policy stasis when interest group demands are stable, group resources are invariant, and partisan control of government (with all that implies for access to politicians by different interests) is unchanging. Yet I contend that even in such circumstances politicians may redirect policy because of revised conclusions about the effects of their choices. It is therefore essential to understand what produces changed beliefs.

I cannot prove my argument with statistical rigor. My data are insufficient to allow for that, especially since I arrived at the notion of the importance of causal stories inductively, from conducting case studies. Nevertheless, I aim to be more systematic and thorough in evaluating the empirical evidence than is typical of the literature stressing the importance of policy deliberation.[2] I offer specific criteria for determining if pressure theory is sufficient to explain choices in the policy area in which I focus, as well as criteria for determining if ideas are important. I evaluate these criteria across jurisdictions and over time.

The second major purpose of this book is to provide further support for the notion that "institutions matter." More specifically, I argue that differences between the American style separation-of-powers system and the Westminster parliamentary system have a large impact on policy decisions. Here I am traveling along a more well-plowed path than I am in emphasizing the importance of causal stories. Recent work by R. Kent Weaver and Bert A. Rockman (1993a) is especially significant

The Issue Focus: Automobile Insurance Reform

in this regard. Their research centers around a set of comparative case studies of policy decisions by the national governments of first world democracies. Based on the case studies, Weaver and Rockman conclude that differences between a parliamentary and a separation-of-powers system matter for policy in specified ways, although the effects are conditional on a number of other factors. Yet this conclusion is offered tentatively, with due respect for the small number of governments examined.

My study goes beyond the work of Weaver and Rockman in two ways. First, by drawing on new data from a different level of government (i.e., a comparison of subnational governments in Canada and the United States), I can provide an independent test for their findings. At the same time, I am able to enlarge the sample and thereby be more confident of the independent role played by institutional differences. This approach is consistent with a suggestion offered by the methodological literature for dealing with the "small N problem" commonly facing political scientists: examine other levels of government to test hypotheses developed from analysis conducted at one level (King, Keohane, and Verba 1994). Second, I expand upon earlier explanations of the circumstances in which institutional differences matter by linking these differences to beliefs about policy consequences.

THE ISSUE FOCUS: AUTOMOBILE INSURANCE REFORM

Much comparative public policy research is conducted at arm's length and covers an array of policy issues. Such an approach is appropriate for many purposes. Yet if one is interested in whether and how ideas affect policy choices, it is necessary to get closer to how policymakers themselves think. And if the researcher is especially interested in beliefs about policy consequences, it is essential to have a relatively sophisticated understanding of the policy area in question. Failure to obtain such an understanding would increase the likelihood of missing or misinterpreting cognitive frameworks that affect people's judgments.

Naturally, obtaining a deeper understanding of a policy area requires specialization. I have therefore chosen a research strategy that is broad in terms of jurisdictions considered and amount of information gathered about policymakers' choices, but narrow in terms of issue focus. I concentrate on a single issue: automobile insurance reform. The jurisdictional universe for this study consists of the fifty American states and ten Canadian provinces, and the time focus is the mid-1980s through the mid-1990s.[3] This approach permits me to be relatively certain that I understand the substantive policy questions well, while allowing me to make a large number of comparisons. The tradeoff is a potential loss of external validity. I discuss this issue further in the final chapter. For now, suffice it to say that I believe such a tradeoff is worthwhile.

Why should one study automobile insurance reform? Quite simply, I believe it is a wonderful issue for examining the role of political pressure, ideas, and institutions. Automobile insurance may not engender the moral fervor that does an issue such as abortion. However, any issue that affects the all-but-sacred ability of North Americans to operate their cars can still generate plenty of passion and resultant pressure on lawmakers. Major interest groups invest heavily in this issue as well. The policy community offers piles of information and clear policy alternatives.

Perhaps most significant of all, decisions on automobile insurance reform constitute a natural experiment in two important ways. First, jurisdictions all across the United States and Canada began with the same means for handling damage recovery in automobile accidents: the tort system. Hence any moves away from tort and toward a no-fault system (probably the most widely considered major reform option in both countries) create special opportunities for comparative assessment of the influence of different political factors. Second, while the nature of the auto insurance reform issue is strikingly similar across the two countries, Canadian and American political institutions differ sharply. Thus scholars can observe the effects of the different approaches to republican government that took hold on each side of the forty-ninth parallel.

More specifically, some of the notable features of the issue are highlighted below.

Automobile Insurance Reform Has Been a Major, Controversial Policy Issue in Many North American Jurisdictions

Over the past fifteen years, automobile insurance has at times been atop the policy agenda in many different subnational jurisdictions. Influential interest groups have staked out sharply different positions on the issue. Fierce, well-funded political battles have occurred over reform proposals, and political careers have been affected by policy choices. Consider the following examples.

- After unsuccessful efforts to achieve major changes in the state legislature, a total of five popular initiatives pertaining to automobile insurance reform were placed on California's November 1988 ballot. With the insurance industry and trial lawyers making vast infusions of resources aimed at influencing the outcomes

The Issue Focus: Automobile Insurance Reform

on the insurance measures ($37 million was expended on a single unsuccessful measure backed by the insurance industry), campaign expenditures on California's ballot initiatives exceeded the total amount of funds spent nationally by the candidates for the 1988 presidential campaign.[4]

- The issue of how to deal with spiraling automobile insurance costs dominated the 1987 provincial election campaign in Ontario. After the Liberal Party's victory, buoyed by Premier David Peterson's promise of a "specific plan to lower rates," the issue was the subject of intensive discussions among top governmental officials. These discussions led in turn to enactment of major no-fault insurance legislation. A subsequent government contemplated a sharply different approach to automobile insurance reform (establishing a public insurance system), but ultimately backed away from this plan.
- After a multiyear battle, Pennsylvania governor Robert P. Casey in 1990 succeeded in obtaining enactment of comprehensive automobile insurance reform legislation. In an interview shortly before his retirement, Casey indicated that this was one of his proudest accomplishments since the legislation addressed the "biggest consumer issue in the state."[5]
- In 1988 Manitoba's governing New Democratic Party (NDP) lost a vote of confidence and subsequently suffered electoral defeat at the hands of the Progressive Conservative Party. Both losses were widely attributed to anger at the NDP for political manipulation of insurance rates under the province's public automobile insurance system. In 1993 the Progressive Conservatives pushed through their own insurance plan, completely restructuring the existing system.

It is not difficult to determine why automobile insurance reform has been atop the policy agenda. Automobile insurance is a genuine "lunch box issue," of concern to the general public. Given that a car is generally considered a necessity in both Canada and the United States, and that automobile insurance is an actual or virtual legal requirement in all jurisdictions, citizens naturally turn to their elected representatives when they have concerns about the automobile insurance system.[6] This is especially the case when insurance premiums are rising rapidly, as occurred in many places during the latter part of the 1980s and the early 1990s. Such increases prompted widespread demands for reform.

The consequence of the public's concern is that politicians have a strong incentive to succeed with respect to major changes in the automobile insurance system. If a "reform" is effected but rates continue to rise, people will notice. If rates are kept artificially low and companies respond in a way that makes insurance difficult to obtain, many complaints will be forthcoming. Legislatures take (or fail to take) many actions that cause barely so much as a ripple within the general public. At least under some circumstances, people attend to decisions about automobile insurance.

The Complexity of the Issue Makes Plausible Differences in Beliefs about Policy Effects

Suppose that policymakers wanted to reduce the price of automobile insurance for ordinary citizens without major adverse consequences. What should be done? The policy issue is complex enough to allow for both uncertainty and disagreements in answering this question. Answers may depend on views about the nature of the insurance industry (e.g., its competitiveness), the incentives facing companies, the driving behavior of motorists, the nature of losses that tend to be sustained in automobile accidents, the incentives facing insurance claimants, the role of third parties (lawyers, medical providers, automobile repair shops), and many other factors.

Furthermore, there in fact exists a sophisticated policy community that produces voluminous information relevant to evaluating the consequences of policy choices. Among others, this community consists of academic insurance economists, think tanks (e.g., RAND), researchers and actuaries within insurance companies, staff from insurance trade associations, attorneys and law professors concerned about tort laws, members of certain consumer groups, and (in some jurisdictions) professional staff within regulatory agencies. The outputs from this community are widely varied, ranging from highly technical academic articles to reports couched in everyday language designed to be read by a lay audience. Within the past decade, the RAND Corporation alone has produced a number of reports on the effects of adopting no-fault insurance systems. Whether and how elected officials consider such materials are key questions I will address. Clearly, however, this is not a policy area which is lacking in information about the effects of policy choices.

Major Policy Decisions Are Made at the Subnational Level

If one wishes to study choices made by subnational governments, one must concentrate on areas where such governments have considerable freedom to set policy. Automobile insurance is an ideal issue for this purpose. In both the United States and Canada, regulation of automo-

Separation-of-Powers versus Westminster System   7

bile insurance is primarily under the purview of the subnational governments; the respective national governments exercise relatively little policy influence. Consequently, the actions of subnational governments can rightly be considered independent from the desires of higher level authorities.

Pressure Theory Explanations Dominate the Existing Literature on Insurance Politics

By emphasizing the importance of beliefs about policy consequences, I am not simply reiterating the common wisdom about the determinants of public policy in a specific issue arena. In fact, the existing literature on automobile insurance politics indicates that decisions can be sufficiently understood as the product of varying pressures by interested groups. Public policy is seen as the outcome of competition among insurance companies, trial lawyers, consumer groups, etc.

I do not wish to deny the importance of interest group demands. Paraphrasing my graduate school mentor, to do so would be the equivalent of writing about World War II without acknowledging that bullets were fired.[7] Instead, my contention is that we miss a big part of the explanation for policy choices by concentrating only on interest group pressure and ignoring politicians' beliefs.

THE INSTITUTIONAL FOCUS: SEPARATION OF POWERS VERSUS WESTMINSTER SYSTEM

Subnational governments in North America differ in a number of institutional respects. Some jurisdictions (e.g., California, Ontario) have legislatures that are highly professionalized, while others (e.g., Rhode Island, Nova Scotia) have legislatures that are part-time and nonprofessionalized.[8] Some American states (though no Canadian provinces) permit voters to determine policies directly through the ballot initiative process, while others have no direct democracy mechanisms. Virtually all American states have a bicameral legislature, but Nebraska has a unicameral legislature. Some Canadian provinces (e.g., Manitoba) require legislative committee hearings on pending bills, while others do not.

Yet while some institutional differences exist within and even overlap national boundaries, the most profound distinction is between the governments of the fifty American states and the ten Canadian provinces. This distinction is stark and consistent (see especially Moncrief 1990, 1994). All American states use a separation-of-powers system modeled after that of the U.S. national government.[9] The governor, as chief executive, is elected independently of state legislators. Divided government, where a governor of one party faces a legislature controlled by the other party, is not only a theoretical possibility but a common occurrence (Fiorina 1992). By contrast, all ten Canadian provinces use a parliamentary system modeled after the British House of Commons (the Canadian national government uses such a system as well). The chief executive, or premier, is selected from the provincial legislature, as are the ministers with responsibility for overseeing governmental agencies.

The institutional distinction is sharpened because the Canadian provinces (and American states) use first-past-the-post electoral rules to select legislators, rather than proportional representation. It is generally understood that proportional representation tends to broaden the number of parties represented in parliament and commonly leads to coalition governments. Under proportional representation, parliamentary systems may come to resemble the separation-of-powers system used in the United States in that interparty negotiation may often be required to secure enactment of legislation. By contrast, the Westminster system characteristic of the Canadian provinces, with its plurality method of selecting lawmakers, tends to produce majority government and minimize the need for interparty bargaining.[10] Given vigorous competition among more than two parties in some provinces, minority government remains possible; Ontario produced such a government in the middle of the 1980s, for example. Yet this is far from the norm.

Other characteristics of the two countries' political systems reinforce the primary distinction. Political parties in Canada have developed clear norms of unified action. According to Graham White and Gary Levy (1989), party discipline in the provinces is strong, even compared with other parliamentary systems. By contrast, party discipline in American state legislatures is generally considered relatively weak. This condition has been abetted by various reform efforts, such as the move to primary elections to select party nominees for legislative seats. Additionally, the fact that all Canadian provincial legislatures are unicameral eliminates the need for one type of negotiation (i.e., bargaining between the two legislative chambers) that is commonly required in the United States to effect policy change.

The sharp divergence in political systems makes comparisons between Canadian and American subnational governments especially appropriate for assessing the role of institutions. Furthermore, the relatively similar cultures of the two countries and the extensive cross-border commercial connections make it easier to isolate the institutional factor in accounting for policy differences.[11] Consider factors relevant to public policy toward automobile insurance. As suggested earlier, both countries share a similar "car culture." Additionally, many of the same players are active on both sides of the border. Some of the major insurance companies operate in both countries. Even consumer advocates have crossed the national boundary. Thus, the prominent American consumer advocate Ralph Nader not only appeared in various American state capitals over the past ten years to push his own approach to automobile insurance reform but appeared in Toronto to make a case to the Ontario government as well.

DATA SUMMARY

In the appendix I provide a detailed description of my data sources, but it is appropriate to provide a summary at this point. For the jurisdictions in which I conducted case studies, I draw information from interviews, surveys, direct observation of decision-making processes, government reports, primary source materials concerning policy decisions (e.g., newspaper articles), materials prepared by interested parties (e.g., insurance companies), and previous case studies conducted by other researchers. Information is more extensive for some jurisdictions than for others. For analysis of all states and provinces I draw upon my own binational surveys of insurance policymakers and the insurance "policy community." These surveys were conducted in 1995. I also make use of publicly available data about the insurance industry. Such information is more comprehensive for the American states than for the Canadian provinces because the National Association of Insurance Commissioners in the United States makes an especially vigorous effort to obtain and summarize a variety of types of comparative data.

ORGANIZATION OF THE BOOK

To this point I have given only passing attention to different theories of policy making. In chapter 2 I consider that topic in more depth, focusing on the distinction between theories emphasizing political pressure and theories emphasizing the politics of ideas.

The next part of the book contains the empirical analysis. In chapter 3 I outline two major stories that guided judgments about how well different automobile insurance reform options would work, along with providing contextual information necessary to fully understand the choices faced by politicians. I further contend that one story was much more reasonable than the other, which has implications for appropriate public policy. In chapters 4, 5, and 6 I provide in-depth case studies of battles over automobile insurance reforms in three jurisdictions. Chapter 4 reviews the reform process in Pennsylvania that culminated in enactment of the Casey proposal. Chapter 5 considers an unsuccessful reform effort in Rhode Island. The end of the chapter focuses on differences between Rhode Island and Pennsylvania. Chapter 6 analyzes the series of proposals considered and enacted in Ontario since the middle of the 1980s, with special attention to adoption of no-fault legislation in 1990. In chapter 7 I look beyond the case study jurisdictions for further evidence as to the importance of institutional characteristics. My main argument is that the Canadian parliamentary system made it easier to impose the losses necessitated by major automobile insurance reform than did the American separation-of-powers system.

Finally, in chapter 8 I summarize the arguments made in earlier chapters. I also move beyond automobile insurance and draw implications for policy making in other areas.

My single-minded focus on automobile insurance reform may seem rather daunting to some. Surely there are limits to how much detail people wish to absorb about any issue—even one that an "outsider" (such as myself, when I began examining this particular topic) can find fascinating. Let me assure anyone with such concerns that it is unnecessary to become an "insurance junkie" to make sense of this book. While the policy specifics are important to my analysis, my emphasis remains on politicians and their decisions. In return for a limited investment in understanding a particular issue, my hope is that the reader will receive a more general payoff in the form of an enriched way of thinking about the choices elected officials make, and an enhanced sense of the importance of institutional differences.

NOTES TO CHAPTER 1

1. Notable works of this sort that examine specific policy choices include Derthick and Quirk 1985; and Mucciaroni 1995; more generally, see Bessette 1994; Kelman 1987; Krehbiel 1991.

2. For a summary of much of this literature, especially in the area of legislative politics, and a critical perspective on its empirical weaknesses, see Lascher 1996.

3. It should be noted that the District of Columbia in the United States also operates in many ways like a state, and the sparsely populated Yukon and Northwest Territories in Canada function much like provinces. I ignore these jurisdictions for purposes of this study, however.

4. Source: Public Affairs Research Institute of New Jersey, "140 Million Spent on Citizen Initiative Questions," press release, 13 March 1995. The presidential campaign figure referenced in the main text does not include "soft money" expenditures.

5. Source: interview with the author, 13 September 1994.

Notes to Chapter 1

6. A variety of evidence supports the conclusion that both Americans and Canadians are very attached to their automobiles. For example, recent data indicate that in the United States about 67 percent of citizens are licensed drivers, whereas in Canada about 66 percent of citizens hold driver's licenses. Also, in the United States there are about fifty-five passenger cars for every one hundred people, while in Canada there are about forty-six passenger cars for every one hundred people (source: California State Automobile Association; I am grateful to Robert Burke of CSAA for providing me with this information).

7. This metaphor comes from Raymond Wolfinger.

8. For a recent summary of the professionalization status of American state legislatures, see Rosenthal 1998; for such a summary for Canadian provincial legislatures, see Fleming and Glenn 1997.

9. The decision to opt for a separation-of-powers system may be viewed as the voluntary choice of a state polity, if one that is subsequently very difficult to change. While the U.S. Constitution requires that states adopt a "republican form of government," it does not require the separation of powers. Indeed some have recommended that specific states consider moving toward a parliamentary system; see for example Cain and Persily 1995.

10. For a similar discussion of variance among parliamentary systems and how this can blur the distinction between such systems and separation-of-powers arrangements, see Weaver and Rockman 1993a.

11. Some empirical evidence suggests that even differences in values commonly assumed to separate Americans and Canadians, such as distinctive attachments to equality and individualism, may actually be overstated; see Sniderman, Fletcher, Russell et al. 1996.

2
Explaining Policy Choices: Pressure versus Ideas

> The quantity and quality of information available to legislators is such that they must choose policies whose consequences they cannot fully and perfectly anticipate.
>
> —Keith Krehbiel (1991, 20)

Political scientists and other scholars have offered a variety of theories as to why policies differ across jurisdictions and over time. While no simple classification system can do justice to the range of such theories, it is useful to differentiate between two broad types. "Pressure theory" stresses the influence brought to bear on policymakers by interest groups and others. By contrast, the "politics of ideas" emphasizes what policymakers learn about the consequences of policy alternatives.

How might each type of theory explain policy differences in an area such as automobile insurance reform? The goal of this chapter is to answer that question. I begin by examining pressure theory. Although this theory has become much more sophisticated over time, it retains its emphasis on an essentially reactive role for policymakers, most notably legislators. While modern pressure theory helps to explain policy choices, I contend that it is insufficient. Attention to the politics of ideas is needed as well.

Next I discuss how various scholars have seen ideas affecting policy choices. Much can be learned from earlier work, some of which is exemplary. Nevertheless, I argue that a great deal about the role of ideas remains sketchy. In particular, I contend that inadequate attention has been given to how belief in different causal stories influences decisions.

Suppose I am correct (or for that matter, incorrect) that pressure theory is inadequate to explain real-world outcomes. The issue still remains as to how that could be shown empirically. I address that issue in the last part of this chapter.

PRESSURE THEORY

By pressure theory I am referring to explanations of policy choices entirely in terms of responses to the demands of actors other than elected officials themselves.[1] Pressure theory has a long history in both political science and public choice economics. For example, the pluralist tradition that dominated political science for many years prior to the 1970s reflected a pressure theory view of politics. Public choice theorists (including both political scientists and economists who operate within this tradition) ostensibly make elected officials more central to their analysis, emphasizing that they are rational, goal-seeking actors. Yet much—if not most—of the work in this area can accurately be described as pressure theory. Politicians are commonly assumed to have the same utilitarian goal: reelection or some related notion of political advancement. To the extent legislators' thinking plays a role in decision making, it is a limited one. That is, consideration may be given to the extent to which politicians are aware of demands and the means they use to weigh conflicting interests. Particularly if elected officials are assumed to be aware of what groups want and to weigh demands in a similar manner, the views of the lawmakers themselves can be (and are) ignored. That is, public choice explanations often are reduced to consideration of what external actors want from politicians (see for example Stigler 1971, Peltzman 1976).

For my purposes, it is significant that pressure theory explanations are common in the literature on the politics of government regulation generally, and regulation of the insurance industry specifically. One of the earliest and most famous versions is "capture theory," associated with the work of George Stigler and others.[2] Capture theory emphasizes that economic producers with intense self-interests in policy outcomes will be advantaged in the political process and be able to obtain regulation that provides them with economic benefits (the term "capture" refers to the notion that regulators do the bidding of the very industries they are supposed to control). Lawmakers will perceive it to their advantage to cater to producers, even at the expense of their constituents as a whole, because the latter will pay minimal attention. The theory purports to explain such phenomena as the advent of regulatory control over professional qualifications, which has the effect of reducing entry and allowing those already within the professions to obtain greater income. Applied to insurance, capture theory implies that regulation in this area will tend to reflect the demands of insurance companies.

Empirical analysis has not been kind to capture theory as an explanation of public policy in the insurance realm (or, for that matter, as an explanation of public policy in many other realms; see Mucciaroni 1995; Quirk 1990). In particular, Kenneth Meier (1988, ch. 7) examined a broad range of insurance regulatory policy in the American states and found no support for the notion that the insurance industry dominates the policy-making process. Additionally, Stephen D'Arcy (1982) studied the effect of intensity of regulation on profitability in the property-liability industry and found that capture theory did not adequately explain regulatory behavior.[3] Some research even has indicated that the insurance industry, and notably the automobile insurance line, is plagued by "rate suppression," i.e., a situation in which regulators tend to hold rates below what they would be in a nonregulated market (Harrington 1993). This is the opposite of the "pro-industry" result that capture theory predicts.

Yet the demise of the capture model has not led to the abandonment of pressure theory. Instead, pressure theory has become more subtle and complex. Consideration is often given to the competing demands of interested parties other than insurance companies (e.g., attorneys), as well as to fissures within company ranks. Meier (1988), for example, essentially offers a pressure theory explanation of policy choices, but with relevant pressure assumed to come from a wide variety of sources.

To illustrate more precisely how contemporary versions of pressure theory explain policy choices, I will concentrate in depth on two important works that use this approach. The first is Scott E. Harrington's (1994) analysis of decisions to enact no-fault automobile insurance laws in the American states during the 1970s. There are four reasons to examine this piece. First, it pertains to the area of insurance regulation that is the substantive focus of my book. Second, it is written by a major figure within the insurance policy community (Harrington is a former president of the American Risk and Insurance Association). Third, it is exceptionally clear and uses rigorous empirical methods. Fourth, it is of recent vintage.

Harrington's model for explaining differences in policy choices is driven entirely by variance in pressures external to state legislatures. Harrington explicitly postulates that lawmakers everywhere have the same goal of maximizing political support and implicitly argues that legislators all use the same means of achieving this end: catering to the perceived desires of different groups, in accordance with their size and the intensity of their demands. He specifies the groups that are most affected by no-fault legislation, including automobile insurance consumers, medical providers, different types of insurance companies, and attorneys. He carefully summarizes their stakes in this issue. He then offers proxy measures for measuring group demands (e.g., premium growth as an indicator of the intensity of consumer demand for lowered premiums; attorneys per capita as an indicator of the size of

Pressure Theory

the lawyer community concerned about the adverse impact of restrictions on tort actions). He finds significant relationships between decisions to adopt no-fault laws and extent of pressure from a number of groups.

If Harrington's article illustrates well the pressure theory perspective, the end of his article inadvertently suggests the limitations of this approach. After showing a positive relationship between consumer pressure and decisions to adopt no-fault laws in the 1970s, he notes that "rapid premium growth in many states in the 1980s did not produce another wave of no-fault laws" (1994, 291). He goes on to speculate that "[t]he fact that some existing no-fault laws have done little to reduce premiums may have weakened the historical relationship between premium growth and public pressure for no-fault." In short, he implicitly argues for the potential importance of social learning within the general public.

But is this the most reasonable place to locate any potential learning effects, given what is well known about the general public's lack of information about and inattention to specific policy alternatives? Might it not be more reasonable to deduce that *legislators* had (rightly or wrongly) grown suspicious about whether no-fault would produce desired consequences for consumers? Might not lawmakers' access to policy information and investment in analyzing alternative courses of action be critical factors?

More generally, pressure theory tends to ignore a key distinction recently emphasized by students of legislative politics: that between policy choices and policy outcomes (Arnold 1990; Bianco 1994; Krehbiel 1991). Pressure theory essentially assumes that elected officials are judged (and/or believe that they will be judged) solely on the basis of whether their actions correspond with groups' demands at the time policy decisions are being considered. Elected officials are rewarded/punished depending on the positions they take. This ignores the possibility that politicians may be judged after the fact on the basis of whether policy choices led to desirable outcomes (e.g., "Did insurance rates go down after you passed that no-fault bill?"), regardless of what pressures were exerted at the time a decision was made. Yet if this is a serious possibility, even purely self-interested politicians ought to be concerned about how to determine the consequences of different options.

Pressure theory also seems curiously divorced from how policy alternatives are framed in the real world. Those who follow legislative debates closely know that in pressuring legislators to make particular decisions, interest groups seldom limit their claims to what is best for their own members. Instead, groups commonly attempt to influence lawmakers' perceptions of what is best for some wider community

(Rosenthal 1993, 193–95). For example, as I will show in more depth in the case study chapters, attorneys frequently argue that passage of no-fault automobile insurance laws will harm consumers, who will be angry about their inability to obtain full recovery in many automobile accidents and frustrated by no-fault's failure to lower premiums.

Of course, pressure theorists might argue that such arguments are nothing more than gloss, dismissed out-of-hand by lawmakers who remain focused on the strength of group demands. But this type of argument prompts questions that are difficult to answer within the pressure theory rubric. First, when different interest groups make competing claims about what some larger public (e.g., consumers) is demanding, and when it is difficult to tell who represents that larger public, how are legislators to determine who is right? Second, given that interest groups are themselves presumed to be rational actors concerned about efficient resource allocation, why would they bother to make substantive arguments about the impact of policies beyond their own members? If groups knew such claims would be dismissed, would they not do better merely conveying messages of intense member demands?

Interestingly, the limitations of traditional pressure theory are also underscored by perhaps the most sophisticated version of this approach offered in recent years: R. Douglas Arnold's (1990) theory of congressional decision making. Like traditional pressure theorists, Arnold begins with the notion that legislators are motivated foremost by the desire to be reelected. Unlike traditional pressure theorists, Arnold emphasizes the distinction between policy positions and consequences. He further argues that citizens commonly judge legislators on the basis of the effects of their decisions. Citizens may not clearly articulate their sentiments until such effects are apparent. Thus lawmakers have strong motivation to think carefully about the consequences of their policy choices.

More specifically, Arnold stresses the concept of *traceable* effects.[4] He argues that even normally inattentive citizens can judge an individual legislator's performance through "retrospective voting" when there are (a) perceptible changes in the real world, (b) identifiable government actions that citizens believe caused the change, and (c) visible actions (e.g., a roll-call vote) that link lawmakers to the government action. (It should be noted that, with minor wording changes, the same logic would hold for judging a political party under a strong party system.) Furthermore, potential challengers and other political actors stand ready to promote awareness of traceable effects among average citizens. Legislators are well aware of this potential for ex–post-facto performance "audits." Hence, representatives work hard to anticipate when their actions will be traceable and worry about activating the concerns

The Politics of Ideas

of large, diffuse groups such as consumers. Lawmakers will be more likely to see actions as traceable when the linkage between policy positions and outcomes is perceived as uncomplicated. The opposite perception will encourage lawmakers to believe that activation is unlikely.

What determines legislative policy decisions? Arnold (1990, 84) writes:

> To reach a decision, then, a legislator needs to (1) identify all the attentive and inattentive publics who might care about a policy issue, (2) estimate the direction and intensity of preferences and potential preferences, (3) estimate the probability that the potential preferences will be translated into real preferences, (4) weigh all these preferences according to the size of the various attentive and inattentive publics, and (5) give special weight to the preferences of the legislator's consistent supporters.

This list may seem unrealistically demanding. However, Arnold anticipates that real-world lawmakers will make extensive use of shortcuts, such as cues from colleagues.

Arnold thus draws a picture of lawmakers who care about policy consequences, if only because they are worried about activating inattentive groups; his emphasis on such effects brings him closer to the "politics of ideas" camp. Nevertheless, the driving force in his model remains political pressure, in the form of variance in traceability, which affects the amount of pressure that can be anticipated. He leads us to expect that lawmakers will do one thing if decisions are highly traceable (i.e., bend toward diffuse, less attentive groups) and another thing if decisions are not highly traceable (i.e., bend toward special interests that carefully monitor legislative proceedings).

Yet this begs a couple of questions: What will lawmakers do if they face multiple policy options in a particular policy area and their choices are equally traceable under any option? If policy choices can be traced in the same way, why would a set of lawmakers in one jurisdiction make a different decision than a set of lawmakers in another? Arnold's theory does not help us answer such questions. To do so, we need to turn away from pressure theory and toward the literature on the politics of ideas.

THE POLITICS OF IDEAS

Pressure theory is not the only way to explain divergent policy choices. A growing literature on deliberation and what I will term "the politics of ideas" stresses policymakers' understanding of policy consequences.[5] This literature (see for example Bessette 1994; Kelman 1987; Krehbiel

1991) commonly suggests that political institutions such as legislatures are designed to help policymakers assess the effectiveness of alternative policies. (Institutions may also shape how policymakers *value* different outcomes, but I will give less attention to that topic.) Groups of lawmakers and other policymakers may differ on their ideas about "what will work," in part because institutions differ.

The politics of ideas literature indicates there are two main reasons why decision makers care about policy consequences. For one, decision makers want to make "good public policy" (Fenno 1973 is a seminal work emphasizing this motive). A number of empirical studies have found that lawmakers are strongly guided by their own notions of what constitutes desirable policy, even regarding some policies that prompt salient constituency concerns, such as flag burning (Lascher, Kelman, and Kane 1993). Lawmakers may pursue good public policy because it is intrinsically rewarding, helping them derive meaning from their legislative activities (see especially Muir 1982). Legislators may also build sufficient political capital to pursue at least some policy goals without worrying about electoral repercussions (cf. Fenno 1978; Kingdon 1989).

Decision makers may also have more selfish reasons for acting on their understanding of policy consequences (see especially Krehbiel 1991). Notably, constituents may punish legislators for actions that bring undesirable effects, while rewarding choices that lead to desirable effects. In this sense at least an argument about the importance of ideas is consistent with Arnold's (1990) emphasis on lawmakers' worries about being "audited."

The significant thing is that *both* concerns about making good public policy *and* desire to advance political careers may motivate people to act on their ideas about policy consequences. Nor is there any reason to think that these two motives generally will be in conflict. Consider the lessons that can be drawn from the empirical literature on legislative politics. This literature tends to suggest that—although there are some notable exceptions—lawmakers commonly do not perceive a conflict between their notions of good policy and what their constituents want them to do (Kingdon 1989).

Yet if much recent literature is articulate in emphasizing the importance of ideas, such literature is generally less helpful in indicating exactly why it is that decision makers adopt one set of ideas rather than another. Indeed, some scholars seem content with merely showing that "ideas matter." We need to go much farther to explain different policy decisions.

Two exemplary works provide a good initial base for identifying key factors: *Information and Legislative Organization* (1991) by Keith

Krehbiel, and *The Politics of Deregulation* (1985) by Martha Derthick and Paul Quirk. Krehbiel's influential work emphasizes the distinction between policies and outcomes, as well as lawmakers' uncertainty about the relationship between them. Such uncertainty is so central to his analysis that he offers it as one of two main postulates from which the remainder of his theory is derived (1991, 15–20). In Krehbiel's account the U.S. Congress (and by implication, modern legislatures generally) are organized to provide expertise to the membership as a whole, thereby increasing lawmakers' confidence in the likely results from the policies they choose. The committee system allows legislators to capture gains from specialization, as particular representatives develop expertise in distinct areas and share their knowledge with their colleagues. Lawmakers engage in a complex "signaling game" that effectively induces participants to share information in an efficient manner.

Krehbiel's analysis is subtle, and aimed at accounting for legislative organization rather than explaining why specific policy decisions are reached. Nevertheless, it is important to note that he essentially offers only a single means by which legislators can determine whether a policy will have desirable consequences: assessing the "balance" (and to a lesser extent the extent of specialization) of the committee that considers a piece of legislation. Lawmakers will be more likely to trust the policy conclusions of a committee that is ideologically balanced (and has a reputation for a high degree of specialization). In other words, Krehbiel suggests that lawmakers determine whether something is a good idea by taking cues from what they already know about the committee that earlier considered that policy choice.

Krehbiel's emphasis on committee membership cues seems reasonable. Yet it also seems insufficient to explain why politicians reach conclusions about the consequences of policy choices. This is especially the case for subnational legislatures, where committee membership is commonly more fluid, and committees have less opportunity to build the type of reputations they do in the U.S. Congress (Rosenthal 1998, 133–45). Naturally, such is also true of Westminister parliamentary systems where legislative committees often are tangential to the main decision-making process. But even in the U.S. Congress, when assessing the consequences of different policy options, we would expect legislators to rely on more than cues from what they know about committee make-up. This is most notably so with respect to committee members themselves.

In the course of explaining the extensive industry deregulation that occurred in the United States during the late 1970s, Derthick and Quirk specify a broader range of methods politicians may use to determine policy consequences. Consistent with the general legislature on legislative decision making (see especially Kingdon 1989), Derthick and Quirk (1985, 119) stress the need for legislators to make such assessments "without investing much effort," given the time pressures lawmakers face and the number of decisions they must make. Instead, legislators rely on "cues on the merits." Such cues relate to both the *sources* and *content* of information/arguments. For Derthick and Quirk the most important cues might be summarized as follows:

- *Source cue 1: expert consensus.* Derthick and Quirk stress that legislators' ultimate support for deregulation rested in part on the diversity and breadth of the group of experts supporting the principle.
- *Source cue 2: support by experts without an interest in the outcome (or with an interest in a different outcome).* Derthick and Quirk contend legislators were influenced by the fact that deregulation was advocated even by some regulatory agencies that might be seen as having an interest in maintaining the status quo.
- *Content cue 1: arguments have an "intuitive" character.* While Derthick and Quirk do not explicate what an "intuitive" explanation entails, it appears they want to argue (1985, 120–21) that such an explanation accords with "common understanding," as did the notion of how deregulation might affect markets.
- *Content cue 2: simplicity/accessibility to lay audience.* Derthick and Quirk (1985, 120) contend that unlike some other economics-based arguments, the intellectual case for the beneficial consequences of deregulation "could be presented simply and effectively in layman's language."

Presumably all these cues might vary across issue options and under different circumstances. Politicians would most likely be convinced of the beneficial consequences of a policy choice if all four were present (as Derthick and Quirk argue was the case for deregulation). On the other hand, policymakers would be skeptical about a policy choice which featured expert disagreement, advocacy only by groups with an interest in the outcome, a nonintuitive rationale, and a justification that was difficult to present to a lay audience.

Building on the work of Derthick and Quirk, it is possible to move farther in identifying "cues on the merits," especially relating to the actual content of policy alternatives. I would suggest that more attention needs to be paid to what I will term *causal stories*. By this I mean broad, integrated accounts of why a public policy problem exists, with implications for what needs to be done to solve the problem. Each story may contain a number of propositions linked together in a coherent manner. Alternative causal stories may "float around" a policy community, just as Kingdon (1995) argues more specific policy alternatives do.[6] Politicians may come to embrace one or another of such stories, and this may heavily influence what course of action they choose.

Cognitive psychology provides some reason to think that people make extensive use of causal stories in making important choices. The "story model" of juror decision making, developed by Nancy Pennington and Reid Hastie (1993a, 1993b), is particularly notable. According to Pennington and Hastie, jurors do not simply evaluate each new argument and new piece of evidence in terms of their overall assessment of which verdict is most appropriate. Rather they first develop a causal story that links together events in the case. Since alternative stories are possible, jurors must settle on one. After they have done so, jurors choose the verdict that best fits the story. In other words, stories serve a significant intermediary role between information and decisions.

If policymakers operate in a similar manner, we might expect that they use stories to synthesize the mass of information made available to them about policy options. A key question then becomes, What prompts policymakers to distinguish among competing stories? The answer to such a question remains uncertain. However, my research (and to some extent the work of Pennington and Hastie) suggests a number of factors that may be important, including the following:

- *credibility of the sources backing the story;*
- *extent to which a story is presented clearly and used consistently by those advocating a policy approach;*
- *simplicity and coherence of the story;* and
- *ability of the story to account for well-recognized "facts."*

Ultimately the extent to which causal stories influence policy choices is an empirical question (if a potentially complex one) as is the question of whether the above-listed factors influence story acceptance. I turn now to criteria for assessing such questions.

ASSESSING THE INFLUENCE OF PRESSURE AND IDEAS ON AUTOMOBILE INSURANCE REFORM

In the empirical chapters of this book, my aims are to provide strong evidence (but not statistical "proof") that (1) pressure theory is insufficient to account for variance in automobile insurance reform decisions,

(2) differences in "cues on the merits" help to account for such variance, and (3) causal stories are an important part of such cues. There are also two types of variance to be explained. For purposes of this study, *longitudinal variance* will refer to major changes in subnational government policy toward automobile insurance policy within a single North American jurisdiction. *Cross-sectional variance* will refer to differences in government policy across subnational jurisdictions at roughly the same time.

If my argument is accurate, we should have the following expectations with respect to automobile insurance reform in the real world:

- Different levels of pressure (e.g., greater or lesser "traceability" of decisions by diffuse groups such as consumers) should be insufficient to explain cross-sectional variance in adoption of insurance reform measures; different levels of pressure (e.g., major groups changing from opposition to support of reform) should be insufficient to explain longitudinal variance in enactment of reform;
- Adoption of major reforms should be associated with cues tending to convince policymakers that such policy changes are likely to work (and failure to adopt such reforms should be associated with the absence of such cues); and
- Evidence of competing causal stories should be found; adoption of some types of reforms should be associated with policymakers' acceptance of a particular story, while failure to adopt reforms (or adoption of very different reforms) should be associated with acceptance of another story.

In assessing the impact of pressure, it is more feasible to rely on relatively objective measures available from "arms length" research (e.g., number of attorneys), as Harrington (1994) does in the article on no-fault insurance discussed earlier. To assess factors relating to the politics of ideas, it is necessary to get closer to the decision makers themselves, and the actual arguments they consider. Therefore there is a compelling need for comparative case studies of decision-making processes in different jurisdictions. In the chapters that follow, I offer such case studies, supplemented with data from multiple jurisdictions, as appropriate.

CONCLUSION

Pressure theory explanations have dominated accounts of public policy in the insurance arena. Nevertheless, there are good reasons for believing that differing views about the consequences of policy alternatives also matter. There is also reason to think that such differences in views may be related to acceptance of causal stories. Subsequent chapters will assess these propositions.

NOTES TO CHAPTER 2

1. For a similar argument about the prevalence and nature of pressure theory, see Quirk and Mucciaroni 1996. Quirk and Mucciaroni use the label "power politics approach," but essentially mean the same thing. I prefer the word "pressure" because I think there is less ambiguity about what it entails and because it best conveys the intuitive meaning of what I see as fundamental to these explanations (i.e., politicians simply respond to outside stimuli).

2. Stigler is widely cited by economists as capture theory's originator, although many political scientists had previously made similar arguments; on this point see Meier 1988, ch. 2.

3. To be fair, D'Arcy found that some competing explanations of regulatory behavior were not adequate either.

4. Arnold himself italicizes this term. For a definition, see Arnold 1990, 47.

5. I have chosen to use the term "politics of ideas" rather than "deliberation," because I think the latter term suggests that policymakers' views are necessarily shaped by a deliberative process within the institutions in which they work (e.g., legislatures). However, policy ideas may *predate* deliberation. For further analysis of what the term "deliberation" does and does not imply, see Lascher 1996.

6. Kingdon's influential work stresses the independence of the "policy stream" and the "problem stream." In this model, solutions (policy options) are attached to problems, but there is not necessarily any interdependence between the two. Yet as Mucciaroni (1992) argues, in many real-world circumstances (including the notable example of American industry deregulation in the 1970s), an explicit link is made between problem diagnosis and possible solutions. This suggests that causal stories are more important than Kingdon may seem to imply.

3
The Profiteering Story and the Pogo Story

> Hit Me—I Need the Money!
> —Popular bumper sticker and title of automobile insurance reform book by Marjorie Berte (1991)

At the heart of this chapter is a claim about how policymakers were likely to view the automobile insurance reform issue. I contend that policymakers tended to embrace one of two causal stories. These stories not only provided diagnoses regarding the nature of the "insurance problem," but offered predictions about what would occur under different policy options. Acceptance of one or the other stories largely determined what policy choice was advocated.

Before outlining the stories, more background is helpful. A basic understanding is needed of how automobile insurance systems have operated in North America. I provide such an overview in the initial section of this chapter. Also, the reader should be convinced that there was a commonly perceived "insurance problem" during the period studied. Such an understanding helps one accept the notion that different views of *why* the problem exists separated people, rather than that different views of *what* the problem was separated people. I provide support for the claim of consensus about the problem. I then briefly describe the various "solutions" that floated in the "policy primeval soup," to use Kingdon's memorable metaphor (1995, 116–17). Next I consider the positions of interest groups that traditionally have staked out positions on the proposed solutions. My aim is to explain who was seen as the likely winners and losers under particular policy choices.

After completing the above tasks, I present the stories themselves. I explain what they imply about policy consequences and what they suggest about the willingness to impose losses on interest groups. Subsequently, I move beyond describing the stories and assess which one actually conforms better with available facts. I contend that one of the stories conforms much better than does the other.

At the end of the chapter, I do one more thing necessary to place the case study chapters in context: I summarize the actual policy changes made by North American jurisdictions during the period covered. This information allows the reader to quickly discern where the case study jurisdictions fit within the broader pattern of decisions about automobile insurance reform.

AN OVERVIEW OF AUTOMOBILE INSURANCE SYSTEMS

I move now to an overview of private passenger automobile insurance systems as they have operated in the United States and Canada. Too much should not be made of use of the plural word "systems." While there are meaningful differences across subnational jurisdictions, there are also many similarities.

The Insurance "Product"

What is it that consumers are purchasing when they obtain automobile insurance? In essence, they are buying some amount of (1) protection against liability for others' losses resulting from an automobile accident (often referred to as "third party" coverage,) and/or (2) entitlement to reimbursement for personal losses resulting from an accident or other mishap involving their own vehicles ("first party" coverage). More specifically, insurers generally offer a package of different coverages under the rubric of a single automobile insurance policy (Cummins and Tennyson 1992). These include *liability insurance*, for third party losses; *personal injury protection*, to compensate for first party accident-related losses (i.e., those sustained by the policyholder, such as foregone wages and medical costs); *collision insurance*, for repairing/replacing the policyholder's vehicle, and *comprehensive insurance*, to cover non-collision-related losses from such sources as theft or fire. Further distinctions are common as well. For example, liability insurance is commonly divided between coverage for injuries to people and coverage for damage to property. Additionally, insurers typically offer specific first party coverage to protect against losses caused by another driver who causes an automobile accident, but is uninsured (or underinsured) and lacks assets sufficient to make compensation. This is known as uninsured motorist coverage.

From a policy perspective, one of the most significant features of automobile insurance, and one that makes it different from virtually all other products offered in the private market, is its compulsory nature. Liability insurance is required to operate a motor vehicle in all Canadian jurisdictions (Insurance Bureau of Canada 1994, 7). J. David

Cummins and Sharon Tennyson (1992, 96) have written that "[l]iability insurance is at least quasi-compulsory in all [American] states," because state laws either require that motorists purchase such insurance or demonstrate proof of their ability to pay claims following an accident. The precise amount of liability coverage that must be purchased varies. Some jurisdictions also require that motorists purchase personal injury protection coverage, often known as "no-fault" coverage. (The no-fault option will be discussed in greater depth later in this chapter.) Collision and comprehensive insurance are optional in all jurisdictions.

Another significant feature of automobile insurance is that even a single provider will tend to offer the same policy at widely varying prices to different customers.[1] This is because expectations of the actual benefits an insurance provider will need to dispense (in the form of claims paid) differ substantially across customer groups. For example, young drivers and motorists living in densely populated urban areas tend to pay more for the same insurance coverage than do other motorists. On average, young drivers are more accident prone, hence more likely to file claims or be the subject of claims by others. Similarly, property losses are more likely in big cities where roads are more congested and theft rates are higher. According to a recent study, the average size of rate disparities for motorists living in cities and those living elsewhere can easily exceed $1,000 annually (Miller 1998).

Private- and Public-Sector Insurance Providers

Automobile insurance usually is provided by private, profit-making firms. These firms vary considerably in size, market share, and clientele. Insurance companies also have different geographic bases, with some operating in only one jurisdiction while others conduct business in a multitude of locations. Indeed, a number of automobile insurance firms, such as Allstate, operate in both the United States and Canada. Additionally, for a great many companies, automobile insurance is just one of a number of lines of insurance that are offered. Automobile insurance providers may also offer homeowners insurance, life insurance, and other types of coverage.

To the extent that automobile insurance is a moneymaking enterprise, profits may come in two forms. First, premium revenues may exceed operating expenses and claims costs. Second, insurance companies earn investment income (although investment income is less important in the auto insurance arena than it is for "long-tail" lines such as life insurance). The potential for such income essentially arises because premiums are paid "up front" while reimbursement for losses occurs subsequently. In the real world, it is generally true that the second mechanism is needed to make automobile insurance profitable; compa-

An Overview of Automobile Insurance Systems

nies usually take an "underwriting loss," i.e., claims costs and expenses exceed premium revenues (Cummins and Tennyson 1992, 101–02). This is not to say that the addition of investment income necessarily makes automobile insurance profitable in any particular time period, because it is possible for underwriting losses to outstrip both moneymaking mechanisms.

The automobile insurance industry is a large one. An estimated $82.8 billion in premiums were generated by the private passenger automobile insurance industry in the United States in 1991 (Insurance Information Institute 1993, 23). The same industry generated $7.9 billion (Canadian) in premiums in 1993 (Insurance Bureau of Canada 1994, 7). Automobile insurance alone accounts for about one-half of all private insurance sold in Canada.

In each of these four Canadian provinces—British Columbia, Manitoba, Quebec, and Saskatchewan—motorists must purchase insurance from a single government-operated corporation (frequently referred to in Canada as a "Crown corporation"). The move to public insurance preceded the 1980s in all four provinces. The public corporations operating in these jurisdictions are intended to be self-sustaining, with premiums generating revenues sufficient to administer the systems and pay claims. In Quebec, the government system covers only bodily injury, while private insurers cover property damage; in the other three provinces, the mandatory governmental system pays for both injury and property losses. Private insurers compete with the public corporations for supplemental and optional coverage in all four provinces.

Government Regulation

Private-sector automobile insurance is a heavily regulated industry in both countries. The regulation primarily occurs at the subnational level rather than the national level. Under the McCarran–Ferguson Act, Congress specifically exempted "the business of insurance" from federal regulation, to the extent that the industry is regulated by the states. According to Jonathan Macey and Geoffrey Miller (1993, 2):

> The McCarran–Ferguson Act is unusual—perhaps unique—in the extraordinary degree of deference it displays toward state regulation. Many federal statutes implement mixed systems of regulation in which states are given a primary role. But few, if any, other statutes expressly assign the states exclusive regulatory jurisdiction over an area of commerce or so closely disavow the role of federal regulation.

In Canada, both federal and provincial governments have a role in regulation, but the federal government's responsibility is limited primarily to ensuring the solvency of insurance companies. Provincial officials determine public policy with respect to coverage that must be offered and engage in any regulation of rates that may occur (Insurance Bureau of Canada 1994, 4).

The restrictiveness of regulation differs substantially across jurisdictions and over time (see especially Meier 1988). For example, in the United States some states (e.g., Pennsylvania) presently have laws that require prior approval from the state insurance commissioner before rates can be changed, while others (e.g., Illinois) allow the open market to determine rates, without regulator intervention. The province of Ontario provides a good example of regulatory change within a single jurisdiction. Prior to 1987, the Ontario government did not regulate rates. In 1987 the government both imposed an across-the-board freeze on premium increases and began to put in place a system for reviewing and approving rate changes (Devlin 1993; O'Donnell 1991).

WHAT WAS THE PROBLEM?

Because subnational governments have gone so far as to require purchase of automobile insurance, they find it difficult to avoid responsibility for "solving" perceived problems with the provision of automobile insurance. And indeed a wide variety of concerns have arisen at different times in North American jurisdictions. Some of the most prevalent concerns about "the insurance problem" that were at least discussed by policymakers in the period I studied are summarized as follows:

- Rates are generally too high. (dominant concern)
- Certain groups of people are paying too much for insurance (e.g., young drivers, big-city residents).
- Insurance is unavailable or unaffordable for certain people (e.g., poor people, drivers who have been in accidents).
- Uninsured motorists are unfairly burdening other drivers.
- Benefits are inadequate for motorists seriously injured in automobile accidents.
- It takes too long to obtain accident benefits.
- There is an unacceptable amount of insurance fraud.

The "insurance problems" listed above vary significantly in their nature and range. Concern about insurance availability and affordability relates mainly to subpopulations, while concern about the general level of rates pertains to the motoring public more broadly. Rates issues relate to the costs of insurance, while concern about payment of accident claims relates to the benefits. Most of the problems listed above are

What Was the Problem?

framed in utilitarian terms, but the concern about uninsured motorists is generally framed as a matter of fairness or justice.

Yet while many concerns arose, to the extent that automobile insurance made it to the agenda of subnational governments, I contend that dissatisfaction with rate levels in general tended to dominate attention. My explanation for this is not complicated. During the 1980s and early 1990s, automobile insurance rates were tending to rise rapidly; average expenditures for automobile insurance grew faster than the rate of inflation during this period. This trend is shown in figure 3.1, which presents data for the American market (a similar trend existed in Canada). As shown in figure 3.1, the gap was especially sharp in the middle 1980s. For example, in 1986 the cost of living (CPI) for all items increased by only 1.9 percent. However, the average price of automobile insurance increased by 13.3 percent.

Such rate increases constitute exactly the sort of changes we would expect to prompt widespread concern by both ordinary citizens and their representatives. For one thing, substantial insurance premium hikes are virtual archetypes of the type of "indicators" Kingdon (1995, 90–115) finds associated with upward movement on the agenda as a result of an issue coming to be defined as a problem. For another, major rate changes fit well with what is known about conditions that make self-interest salient for ordinary citizens. Jack Citrin and Donald Green (1990) have shown that the role of self-interest is enhanced when the consequences of policy choices are visible, tangible, large, and certain. Recent rate increases in many jurisdictions fit these criteria. Additionally, the compulsory nature of insurance made the connection to the public policy arena easy to trace, while the near universally perceived need for an automobile meant that concern would not be limited to subpopulations. Indeed, it might be expected that many citizens essentially viewed rate hikes as "just another tax," and there is strong empirical evidence that self-interest tends to be salient for tax issues (Citrin and Green 1990).

Moreover, it is not difficult to see why the public's concern was focused on rates rather than, say, the adequacy or timeliness of benefits. Rate increases readily manifest themselves in highly visible, quantifiable measures. While some companies may have responded to cost pressures in part by reducing service rather than hiking premiums, such changes were likely to be less readily apparent to the public. Benefit changes were also likely to be less obvious to members of the media who could reinforce the importance of the "rates problem" with stories about this topic, replete with graphs and charts.

The evidence that rate concerns in fact dominated the agendas of subnational governments comes from a variety of sources. Most

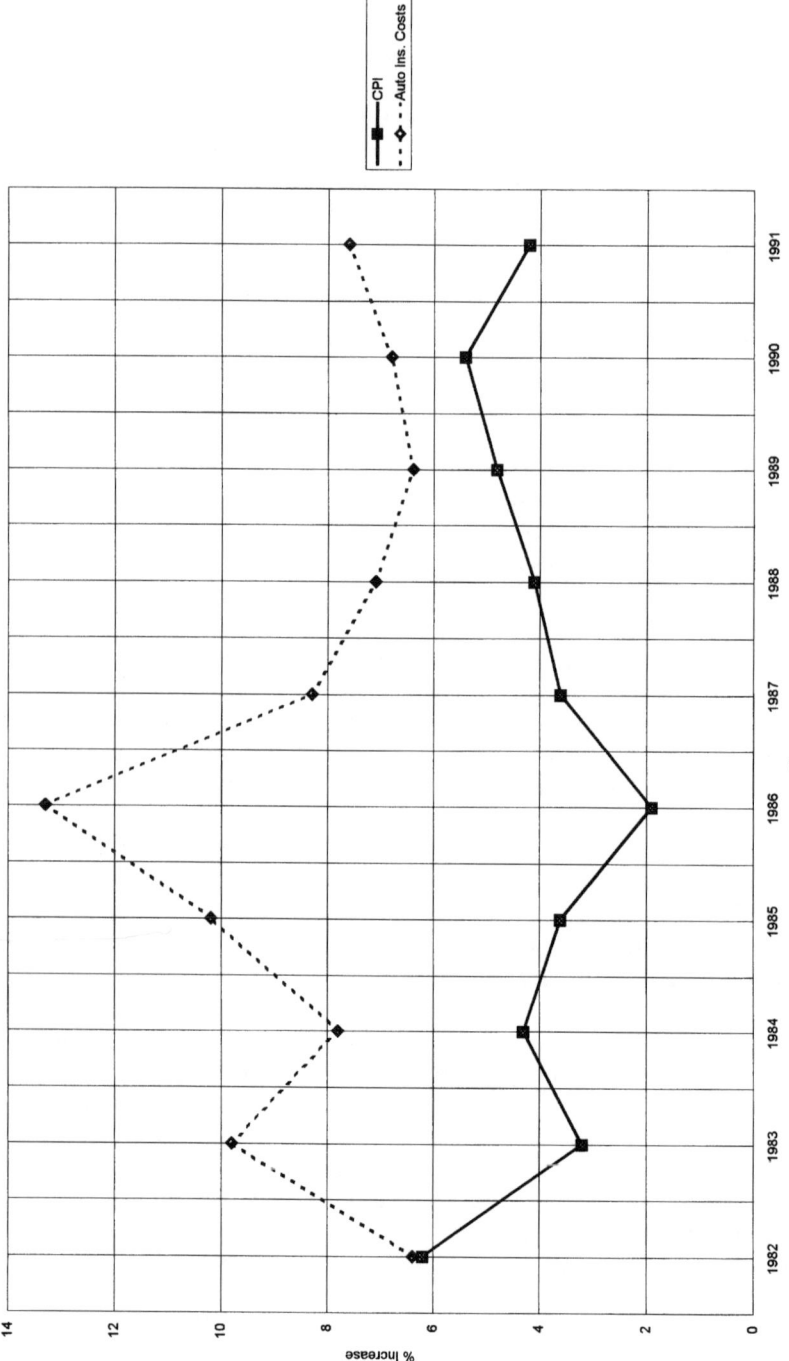

Figure 3.1. Automobile Insurance Premium and Cost of Living (CPI) Trends in the United States, 1982–1991
Source: Insurance Information Institute 1993, 50–51

What Was the Problem? 31

notably, all the case studies of insurance battles in specific jurisdictions I have reviewed indicate as much, regardless of whether I conducted the research or the studies were done by others. My survey of insurance officials in the United States and Canada provides further evidence. The survey responses indicate that either rate concerns were dominant or the insurance issue tended to be off the agenda for elected officials. Below I briefly summarize the findings with respect to the issue agenda in different jurisdictions.

The Agenda in Rhode Island

In late 1992 I began a "real time" study of legislative deliberation and decision making in Rhode Island. My interest in Rhode Island was prompted by signs that the state legislature was "opening up" after a long period of domination by legislative leaders. At the time I began the study I had not yet chosen to focus on the automobile insurance issue; I decided to concentrate on that topic because it appeared to be a major issue for the legislature and because it was a potentially complex issue for lawmakers.

All signs indicated that a concern about high and rising rates prompted the high degree of attention to automobile insurance reform in Rhode Island. In this context, well over half of the more than twenty-five lawmakers I interviewed in the spring of 1993 spontaneously mentioned automobile insurance as one of the most important issues facing the state. Almost invariably, these comments were accompanied by remarks about high and rising premiums, or such comments were offered after I prompted legislators about the nature of the insurance problem. ("We pay too much," one legislator said simply. "Rates have gone through the roof," said another.) Legislators commonly compared insurance costs in Rhode Island to those in other states, citing statistics indicating that average premiums in Rhode Island were among the highest in the nation. The emphasis on premium levels wasn't limited to certain types of legislators, but cut across party lines, divisions between the two houses, and divisions between groups supporting competing proposals for reducing rates. Additionally, journalists, lobbyists, and state regulatory agency officials I interviewed agreed that premium concerns were dominant.

Legislators often made the linkage between the attention given to the rates issue and the concerns of the mass public (as one lawmaker explained, the high insurance premiums "make the public angry and drive the politics of the issue"). One prominent legislator who had been actively involved in this issue explicitly argued that rates were the public's foremost concern, not concern about benefits. Many legislators also indicated that they had gotten a lot of mail and telephone calls from constituents on the insurance issue, although this was not universal.

The Agenda in Pennsylvania

After studying events in Rhode Island, I turned my attention to an earlier automobile insurance reform battle in Pennsylvania which had resulted in a different outcome. Yet while there was divergence in outcomes, I found that the definition of the problem was the same as in Rhode Island. I interviewed people with a variety of perspectives on insurance reform. All agreed that the attention to automobile insurance reform was motivated by the perception that Pennsylvania in general, and metropolitan Philadelphia in particular, had a "rates problem." This impression accorded with available data. In 1989 average total automobile insurance expenditures ranked tenth highest among the fifty states and the District of Columbia, while average expenditures for the liability coverage alone ranked sixth highest (National Association of Insurance Commissioners 1993, 9). One study (Smith and Wright 1992), drawing on a variety of data sources from the late 1980s, indicated that premiums in Philadelphia were the highest among twenty-seven local urban markets. There were no signs of disagreement that public policy ought to have been directed toward making automobile insurance more affordable; the conflict was over how to do this.

The Agenda in Ontario

I next studied the ongoing insurance reform battles in Ontario. I interviewed members and staff of the provincial parliament who were active in public policy on automobile insurance, regulatory officials, insurance company executives, and others involved in the issue. These people were unanimous in indicating that a sudden and dramatic jump in insurance rates in the mid-1980s had moved the issue of automobile insurance to the forefront of the provincial government's agenda (rates had risen nearly 40 percent over a two-year period prior to the spring of 1986; see Baetz 1993). While some mentioned that there was a particular concern about rates for particularly young drivers, all stressed the hike in average premiums. There was further agreement that insurance rates emerged at that time as a potential election issue. In the words of one insurance official, the public had been "radicalized" by the rate hikes and was demanding action.

The information obtained through my interviews is consistent with the conclusions reached by others who have studied the Ontario insur-

What Was the Problem?

ance controversy (see especially Atkinson and Nigol 1989; Baetz 1993; Feldthusen 1990; O'Donnell 1991). Thus Allan O'Donnell (1991, 4) who helped develop the province's no-fault plan, writes that "[c]onsumers reacted with rage because of the double-digit percentage increases" in insurance premiums, and indicates this concern pushed the provincial government to action. Similarly, Bruce Feldthusen (1990, 298) is explicit about the connection between rate concerns and the emergence of automobile insurance as a policy agenda item:

> Consider the political context in which [rate regulation] legislation emerged. In the mid-1980s, the term "insurance crisis" became popular. To the average voter, "insurance" meant auto insurance, and crisis meant higher rates. Most of the anger was directed at insurance companies, courts and lawyers. Nevertheless, the New Democratic Party perceived that a large number of marginal votes might be obtained by a party which promised to rectify the crisis. It made government auto insurance (and lower rates) the keystone of its 1987 election campaign[....] The perception of a crisis, and the NDP's campaign that a government plan would cost consumers less, vaulted the question of auto insurance rates openly onto the public agenda. The minority Liberal government had little choice but to take some action on the issue of rates.

The Agenda in Other Jurisdictions

The objection might be raised that drawing inferences from the case studies is problematic, since the case study jurisdictions are precisely those where rate concerns were most severe, and hence likely to dominate policy debate. This is a reasonable concern. However, evidence from my binational survey of insurance officials indicates that the issue was commonly (although not universally) off the legislative agenda in places where rates were relatively low and/or stable. The attention of elected officials was stirred when insurance rates were rising sharply. Below is a sample of some of the verbatim remarks from survey respondents that confirm this assessment.

- Iowa's auto insurance rates are among the lowest in the country. Auto insurance is not a major concern of the legislature.
  —Iowa Insurance Commissioner
- Auto [insurance] rates [are] quite low and [the] market is stable. [There have been] no real auto issues [in the] last few years.
  —Kansas Insurance Commissioner
- In general, [auto insurance] is a nonissue in [Minnesota]. As a state with a large rural area, [and] generally low accident and crime rates, we have auto insurance rates which are lower than

[those in] most states. Minnesota ranks 22–26 on rate rankings. As a result, auto insurance rates are not a big political issue. —Minnesota legislative staff member
- Automobile insurance rates in Missouri tend to be low. This may account for the lack of legislation.—Missouri legislative staff member
- Ohio has a generally competitive environment with reasonable rates, which is probably why [the no-fault] issue has not received the attention it has been given in other states.—Ohio Insurance Commissioner
- Auto insurance has not been a major—or even minor—political issue in Utah during the '90s[....] The auto insurance market is functioning fairly well in Utah. Our average premiums are lower than the national average[...]—representative of the Utah Insurance Department
- [Automobile insurance is] not a hot political issue in Vermont. [The] public perceives rates as generally reasonable when compared to other Northeast states.—Vermont legislative staff member
- While auto insurance reform has not become the "political football" it has become in Ontario, the Atlantic region is not without issues[.... For example,] the Government of Newfoundland is being forced to consider no-fault as a means to provide relief to customers who have seen rates double over the past four years. —Insurance Bureau of Canada, vice president for the Atlantic provinces (letter)

Interestingly, rates concerns were dominant in the decisions of the Manitoba and Saskatchewan governments to enact sweeping changes to their automobile insurance systems. This is especially notable because average insurance premiums in both provinces were relatively low. Yet in Manitoba worry about sharply rising system claims costs and increasing rates, and the potential for premiums doubling before the end of the century, motivated the government to take drastic action. Similar concern about rising costs motivated the Saskatchewan government to overhaul its insurance system. (See chapter 7 for more details about events in these two provinces.)

POLICY OPTIONS

If "the problem" was that consumers were "paying too much" for automobile insurance, what solutions were available? In theory, there were many. However, as is the case with other policy issues (see King-

Policy Options

don 1995, 116–44) attention commonly focused on options that either seemed obvious or already had been much discussed in the policy community. I summarize major alternatives below. My claim is not that these were the only options that surfaced, but rather that these options frequently dominated the debate.[2]

Rate Freezes and Rollbacks

One option was sufficiently apparent that politicians likely did not need input from the policy community to be aware of it: use government regulatory powers to freeze and/or rollback insurance rates. Insurance providers would be prohibited from charging policyholders more than a specific amount (e.g., the rate levels for the previous year); violators would be forced to provide rebates to customers and might face other penalties. There was no mystery about how such an approach was supposed to aid consumers. The questions that arose concerned whether this approach was sustainable, whether it would withstand court scrutiny (and in particular in the United States, whether it would have violated constitutional prohibitions against the taking of private property without just compensation), how it would be administered, whether exceptions would be allowed, what costs it might entail, whether it would be combined with other measures to reduce the cost of providing insurance, and matters of that sort.

Tight Regulation

A second and related option was to move to a more stringent system of regulating the activities of insurance providers.[3] For example, a jurisdiction might have been operating under a "file and use" system, whereby insurance companies would be required to notify the regulatory agency of rate changes, but would not otherwise be prevented from having them take effect. Such a jurisdiction might have considered moving to a "prior approval" system, whereby the regulatory agency would have to approve rate changes before they could take effect.

The tight regulatory option was likely to be well known to people within the insurance policy community and readily accessible to politicians looking for a potential solution to the rates problem. The regulatory agencies themselves could be expected to be familiar with different regimes, due to extensive information sharing. Summaries of the systems used by different jurisdictions were regularly compiled by umbrella organizations such as the National Association of Insurance Commissioners (NAIC) in the United States. Additionally, there was a straightforward connection between adoption of a tight regulatory regime and addressing the public concern about rates. The clear presumption was that regulators would disapprove unjustified applications for rate increases, thereby saving money for the consumers.

No-Fault Insurance

A third major option was no-fault insurance. The essential features of no-fault insurance as it had evolved in North America, and as it appeared on the agenda for subnational governments, were that 1) some personal injury benefits were to be provided to accident victims regardless of fault, and 2) lawsuits, and especially tort actions to obtain compensation for "pain and suffering," were to be restricted in some manner.[4] Within these broad guidelines a wide variety of permutations were possible. By the late 1980s a number of different no-fault models had in fact emerged and been implemented in different jurisdictions. The policy action in the period I studied consisted both of attempts to adopt no-fault in "traditional tort" jurisdictions and attempts to strengthen existing no-fault systems.

The connection between no-fault insurance and the potential for lower premiums was less readily apparent than was the case for the freeze/rollback and tight regulation options. Absent input from specialists, those without a substantive background in insurance (such as most legislators) might well not have considered the connection. However, many within the policy community were prepared to argue that adoption of no-fault would lower rates by reducing the costs of providing insurance. The cost cuts were seen to result from eliminating some compensation (especially for pain and suffering in minor accidents) and lowering transaction costs, particularly those related to use of the court system. In a well-designed no-fault system these cost savings would more than offset any new costs resulting from the need to pay additional first party benefits.[5] Market pressures would prompt insurance providers to pass along the cost savings to consumers, or regulators might require providers to do so.

While no-fault was commonly offered as a solution to the premium hikes of the late 1980s and early 1990s, no-fault proposals had a life of their own beyond that crisis period. No-fault fits well within Kingdon's (1995, 141) description of "perennials—flowering in one season, then turning dormant, only to flower anew." The idea itself was several decades old. No-fault had been framed as a means of reducing premiums during earlier periods of concern about rates; several American states had adopted no-fault laws in the 1970s with the goal of providing rate relief to consumers (Harrington 1994). Yet no-fault also had been advocated as a means of better ensuring equitable treatment of accident victims, promoting social justice, and achieving other goals. For exam-

Policy Options

ple, Manitoba's left-wing New Democratic Party had backed no-fault because of its consistency with the party's support for protecting all citizens from social harms.[6] Tenacious individual political entrepreneurs also had emerged in support of no-fault. Perhaps none was more notable than American law professor Jeffrey O'Connell, commonly considered one of the "fathers" of the modern no-fault movement. Since the middle of the 1960s O'Connell had continuously pushed for the adoption of no-fault, arguing his case in numerous writings and in many different political arenas.[7]

It is important to note that, by the late 1980s, advocates consistently differentiated among no-fault systems in terms of effectiveness in reducing insurance rates. Advocates even conceded that a poorly designed no-fault system might well lead to rate increases (Carroll et al. 1991). The key to no-fault's effectiveness at cutting costs was seen to be the ability to limit tort claims. It was common to distinguish among the following types of no-fault systems:

- *Monetary threshold no-fault systems* allowed lawsuits only if injured parties' medical losses exceeded a specified amount (e.g., $2,000). These systems were generally seen to provide weak restrictions on legal actions and ineffective means of reducing costs, especially if the threshold was set low (Carroll et al. 1991; Weisberg and Derrig 1992).
- *Verbal threshold no-fault systems* limited lawsuits for pain and suffering compensation (and in some versions, limited all lawsuits) to instances in which accident victims had suffered specified injuries such as permanent disfigurement. These systems were commonly seen as having greater potential for reducing tort actions and overall costs (see for example O'Donnell 1991).
- *Pure no-fault systems* barred all lawsuits. Such systems were often seen as offering the greatest potential for cost savings. As of the late 1980s, Quebec was the only pure no-fault jurisdiction in Canada and the United States. (That was to change in the following decade.)
- *Choice no-fault systems* provided consumers a choice between 1) a traditional tort system insurance policy and 2) a no-fault policy with mandatory first party benefits and some sort of restriction on lawsuits. The potential to reduce costs was seen to depend on both the nature of tort restriction and the proportion of consumers opting for no-fault.

The perceived need to differentiate among types of systems placed additional burdens on no-fault advocates. Supporters often wanted to avoid having politicians lump all no-fault plans together, since that would mean systems seen as likely to work would be tarred by association with systems viewed as unlikely to succeed. I will discuss the implications of this point further when I come to the key stories guiding thinking about automobile insurance reform.

Public Automobile Insurance

A fourth major option surfaced only in Canada; to my knowledge it was never seriously considered in any jurisdiction in the United States. That option was to replace the private-sector automobile insurance system with a single provider public-sector system. According to advocates, such a system would be more efficient, both because there would be no push to derive profits from insurance and because administrative overhead would be lower (e.g., because fewer insurance agents would be needed). Proponents often looked with favor to such places as Manitoba and Saskatchewan, seeing successful, low-cost insurance operations. Among such proponents were leaders of The New Democratic Party (NDP), which had long supported a public system. As will be discussed further in chapter 6, the 1990 advent of the first NDP government in Ontario led to a major battle over public automobile insurance.

INTEREST GROUP POSITIONS

One conclusion is unavoidable: if politicians wanted to address the automobile insurance rates problem by adopting one of the approaches referred to in the previous section, it was virtually certain that losses would have to be imposed on major groups. Consider first the rate freeze/rollback, tight regulation, and public insurance system options. Not surprisingly, insurance companies were hostile to these approaches. Jurisdictions with tight regulatory laws were seen as creating unfavorable business climates (see D'Arcy 1985). Both my case studies and my survey of insurance officials indicate that companies vigorously opposed mandatory freeze/rollback laws wherever they were considered. To cite one specific instance, insurance companies largely bankrolled the losing effort to defeat Proposition 103 in California, which both called for mandatory premium rollbacks and established a tight regulatory regime (Lupia 1994). The insurance industry also waged a fierce and ultimately successful campaign against a public automobile system for Ontario (Walkom 1994).

The no-fault option in turn created its own implacable set of enemies: trial attorneys. It appears to be a universal constant of North American automobile insurance battles that trial attorneys are strongly and vocally opposed to no-fault, in all its various colorings.[8] This resistance is evident in each of the case studies I conducted or reviewed,

Interest Group Positions

as well as in the results of my survey of insurance officials. Within both the existing popular and academic literature on the politics of no-fault, it is also commonplace to emphasize lawyers' virulent opposition (see for example Berte 1991; Dyer 1976; Harrington 1994; Meier 1988; O'Donnell 1991; Spiro and Mirvish 1989).

There are two fundamental bases for trial attorneys' antagonism to no-fault. First, many trial attorneys stand to lose a substantial amount of income from restrictions on tort actions. Automobile accidents are a very important source of tort claims. A 1992 U.S. Department of Justice study indicated that automobile insurance accidents were by far the most common source of state court cases in the nation's seventy-five largest counties, accounting for fully 60 percent of all tort cases disposed (Smith et al. 1995). Second, attorneys tend to have an ideological attachment to protection of "rights," including the unfettered ability to seek redress in the court system (Miller 1995, 17–28).

An interesting question remains as to the stance of consumer groups. The picture here is more complicated than with respect to insurance companies and trial attorneys. In some jurisdictions (e.g., Rhode Island) there were organized consumer groups actively involved in insurance reform battles. In other jurisdictions (e.g., Pennsylvania, Manitoba) there was little consumer group involvement. Furthermore, where consumer groups were active they had been known to take different positions, particularly with respect to no-fault. Some consumer groups supported no-fault. Others, especially those closely associated with Ralph Nader, the famous American consumer advocate, allied themselves with trial lawyers and opposed any restriction on tort claims. Nader himself seemed to have an ideologically based affinity with trial lawyers rooted in his "fondness for product liability suits" (Spiro and Mirvish 1989, 28).

The split between consumer groups recently was evident in California. Voter Revolt, the consumer group which had sponsored Proposition 103, led a successful effort to place a strong no-fault initiative on the spring 1996 primary election ballot. Opposition to the no-fault approach caused one of Voter Revolt's original founders to leave the group. Joining forces with attorney groups and others, he and Nader strongly urged the measure's defeat (*California Journal* 1996). Ultimately the no-fault initiative was soundly defeated by voters.

Yet it appears clear that from the viewpoint of elected officials, input from organized consumer groups was not generally the most noticeable type of consumer demands. Instead, the most forceful input came in the form of spontaneous or loosely organized complaints about high insurance premiums. These included angry correspondence and telephone calls to lawmakers, letters to newspaper editors, statements during talk radio programs, and appearances at political offices. This input was not necessarily linked to any specific policy option, but rather consisted of the demand to "do something" decisive to ease the rate burden. Additionally, politicians could reasonably anticipate that even silent consumers might well express retrospective judgments on success at addressing the rates problem.

Politicians also likely understood that there would be undeniable costs for at least some consumers under some policy options. Most notably, adoption of no-fault would mean that some people injured in accidents would not be able to obtain compensation that they might have obtained under the status quo. This conclusion followed inevitably from the definition of no-fault as it had evolved; proponents did not attempt to deny it.

TWO KEY STORIES

Imagine yourself now in the following circumstances (which, while hypothetical, are designed to reflect the actual ones facing many politicians). It is the early 1990s, and you are an elected official facing impending decisions on automobile insurance reform measures (e.g., a state legislator; a provincial minister or party leader; even a provincial "backbencher" who must determine whether and how to approach party leaders on this topic). You drive an automobile and carry insurance, but have only a cursory understanding of your own insurance policy. It is obvious to you, however, that much of the public is enraged about insurance rates. You would like to address the public's concerns, both because you think it will help you to retain political office and because you believe it is your duty to do so. You are cognizant of a few options, and also well aware that you will have to cross major groups if you support adoption of major changes such as no-fault—it's hard to ignore those groups of lawyers and insurance officials that camped in your office last week. You don't want to adopt a change that will impose significant losses unless you're fairly well convinced that the new policies are likely to work, and you don't want to be surprised by serious ill effects. What will convince you to support one policy solution or another?

I wish to argue that policy choices were influenced by the extent to which politicians accepted one of two causal stories. These were not the only stories possible; they were, however, quite common. The stories served an integrative function, linking together views about the following:

- diagnosis of "how we got into this mess," including identification of any "villains" responsible for the problem;

- explanation for why past efforts to control rates (if any) had failed;
- identification of necessary components for successful reform efforts; and
- predictions of the likely effects of adopting specific plans.

The Profiteering Story

This story revolved around the notion that insurance companies were principally responsible for high and rising rates. The insurance industry was viewed as inefficient, noncompetitive, frequently coddled by regulators, and unaccountable to the public. Insurance executives themselves had caused the run-up in premiums during the time period studied, through profiteering (or partially in an effort to compensate for investment losses). Past efforts to control insurance costs had failed because of the unwillingness or inability of policymakers to take on the industry. Aggressive policies to curb the industry's ability to exploit customers were needed.

If one accepted the Profiteering Story, certain reform proposals matched well and certain ones did not. The rate rollback and tight regulation policy options were a good fit. Public automobile insurance also was consistent with the Profiteering Story, since that option called for completely eliminating the private-sector providers. No-fault plans, however, were seen as failing to address the root of the problem. Furthermore, the Profiteering Story provided a means of explaining information that was commonly highlighted by no-fault foes. This information showed that, on average, insurance rates were actually higher in jurisdictions with no-fault than jurisdictions without it. (See chapter 5 for more detail on use of information of this kind.) Under the Profiteering Story, the reason for this phenomenon was clear: no-fault was tangential to what was necessary to address rates concerns. The Profiteering Story further predicted that enactment of no-fault would lead to consumer disappointment, since automobile accident benefits would be reduced without corresponding rate relief.

The Profiteering Story was most thoroughly articulated by some consumer advocates, such as Ralph Nader. But as I will show in the subsequent case study chapters, this explanation was often floated by others. Some academic commentators have in effect recognized its prevalence as well, without labeling the story as such. Thus in their discussion of the rise in automobile insurance prices in the United States in the 1980s, Cummins and Tennyson (1992, 95, 99) write:

> The populist view is that high insurance costs are primarily attributable to inefficient and excessively profitable insurance companies. Insurers are

accused of paying claims without adequate controls, padding their expenses, and passing the costs along to the consumer, all while being shielded by a federal antitrust exemption[....]

Much of the controversy about the price of auto insurance focuses on the behavior of insurance companies. Many blame insurer collusion for the price inflation of the late 1980s. Others argue that insurers raised prices to current policy-holders to make up for losses experienced in the early to mid-1980s, periods of low profitability.

The Pogo Story (i.e., "We Have Seen the Enemy, and They Are Us")[9]

The essence of the Pogo Story was that "the laws of economics" prompted the perceived crisis in premiums.[10] The insurance industry was seen as highly competitive and profits were not viewed as abnormally high. Sharply rising costs throughout the industry forced insurance providers to raise rates. In particular, steep increases in claims for bodily injury reimbursement placed a financial squeeze on insurance providers.

Perhaps the most striking difference between the Profiteering Story and the Pogo Story was that in the latter consumers themselves (or at least a subset of them) were viewed as significantly responsible for the public policy problem. At minimum, existing insurance systems were seen to provide inadequate incentives against overblown insurance claims. At worst, insurance systems, especially those in traditional tort jurisdictions, were seen to foster a "lottery mentality," whereby accident victims would attempt to secure high pain and suffering reimbursement through padded medical claims. An article in a popular journal (Spiro and Mirvish 1989, 24) captures well this viewpoint, to the point of suggesting that gaming behavior in the automobile insurance arena was more likely to lead to large payoffs than playing traditional government supervised lottery games.

> In America, there are three ways to get rich. You can work hard (but that's no fun). You can win the lottery (perfect—except for the long odds). Or you can get in a car wreck and sue. Due to the publicity that surrounds astronomical jury awards for such dubious injuries as "whiplash," it's this last path to wealth—the fender bender—that sometimes seems to offer the truest promise.

The point about consumer responsibility is also captured in the popular bumper sticker (and title of Marjorie Berte's 1991 book) cited at the beginning of the chapter: *Hit Me—I Need the Money!*

Two Key Stories 43

Consumers were not seen as the only ones responsible. Trial attorneys were viewed as aiding and abetting the tendency to seek court remedies. Attorney advertising was seen to encourage accident victims to file lawsuits, regardless of the nature of the injuries. Unscrupulous medical providers provided a crucial link by showing a willingness to provide unnecessary treatment, thereby strengthening claimants' cases. Insurance companies contributed to the problem through calculated decisions not to challenge suspicious claims because of the expenses involved. While rational on an individual case basis, the aggregate effect of failure to police claims better was that cost pressures increased.

According to the Pogo Story, a means of reducing claims costs had to be found. Strong medicine was needed. No-fault insurance fit well with this view. No-fault posited an explicit trade-off, whereby consumers would give up the opportunity to make certain claims in return for which they would be more than compensated by lower premiums. Rate freezes/rollbacks (unless tied to specific cost reduction strategies) and tight regulation were seen as misguided because they failed to address the underlying cost problem. At worst, these approaches would actually make matters worse for consumers, since providers would respond by contracting the insurance coverage offered or leaving the market (Cheit and Youngwood 1991). Moving to a public system also would not attack the source of the problem, since it simply changed ownership without relieving claims pressures.

Past failures to control rates were seen as the result of watered-down efforts to control costs. Instead of enacting "real no-fault," North American jurisdictions frequently had adopted weak laws that did little to reduce lawsuits (Cheit and Youngwood 1991; Miller 1998; Spiro and Mirvish 1989). The Massachusetts case was seen as exemplary. In 1970 Massachusetts had adopted a no-fault statute with a low monetary threshold ($500 at the time). Because it was easy to incur medical expenses sufficient to pierce the threshold, there had been little impact on lawsuits (Weisberg and Derrig 1992).

Asymmetry between the Two Stories

My argument is that politicians who accepted the Profiteering Story were well on their way to supporting rate freezes, rate rollbacks, and/or tight regulation. Such policymakers also were likely to be more sympathetic to public automobile insurance. Elected officials who accepted the Pogo Story were inclined to support no-fault.

It should be noted that while ideology might influence story acceptance, there was no necessary correspondence between general conservatism and belief in the Pogo Story, nor between general liberalism and belief in the Profiteering Story. A "free market conservative" might commonly advocate for deregulation, but believe that the particular circumstances of the automobile insurance market (e.g., the lack of federal antitrust activity) allowed insurance companies to exploit consumers. An "activist liberal" might think heavy regulation was inappropriate in this specific area.

It is also important to emphasize an asymmetry in the relationship between stories and policy positions. An election-conscious politician might, say, support a rate freeze while not being fully convinced of the Profiteering Story. The rationale would be that such an approach "might work" and, in any event, the consumer benefits would accrue over the short run while any costs (e.g., greater difficulty in obtaining insurance as the result of coverage constriction) would occur over a longer run. On the other hand, the consumer costs of no-fault would begin immediately after implementation. And while some consumers could be expected to be oblivious to this fact, it was not reasonable to expect this would be true across the board. (The scenario a lawmaker might envision is something like this: "Didn't Aunt Marge and Uncle Hank get $30,000 in their little fender bender, before that new law was passed?") The consequence is that it was potentially more important for no-fault supporters to believe the Pogo Story than for supporters of measures such as rate freezes to believe the Profiteering Story.

Was One Story More Reasonable Than the Other?

Thus far I have concentrated on simply describing two common stories, without evaluating their merits. Yet to leave things at that pushes unnecessarily far in the direction of policy relativism. If there is a basis for believing that one story was more reasonable than the other, that is important information. How we evaluate political decision making may in part be determined by whether we believe elected officials "got the story right."[11]

I believe that there are strong grounds for concluding that the Pogo Story was more reasonable than the Profiteering Story. First, the fundamental premises of the Profiteering Story find little empirical support. Consider the assertions about the profitability and lack of competitiveness of the insurance industry. I reviewed data collected by NAIC in the United States, data compiled for investment analysis, government reports from both countries, industry studies, and relevant academic literature. None of this information or analysis supports the notion that the automobile insurance market was noncompetitive, at least defined in terms of firm concentration and ease of entry and exit.[12] Additionally, NAIC data and a number of studies indicate that automobile insurance was not unusually profitable in the late 1980s and early 1990s. Average profits were actually negative in some years during that period.[13]

Second, available information is consistent with the Pogo Story premise of sharply increasing claims pressures, especially with respect to bodily injury coverage. For instance, industry data show that in the United States average dollar losses for bodily injury coverage increased by over 40 percent between 1986 and 1990. During the same period losses for property damage rose by less than 17 percent (NAIC 1993). Consistent with the notion that enhanced use of the court system was partially responsible for increasing losses, studies also found that the portion of injury victims represented by attorneys had risen sharply over time (All-Industry Research Advisory Council 1988).

Perhaps the most striking support for the Pogo Story comes from the Canadian public insurance systems. Consider how the Profiteering Story might have attempted to explain the data referred to in the paragraph above: fat, lazy, unaccountable insurance companies had become increasingly lax about monitoring claims. Even if such an explanation could plausibly have been applied to private-sector firms (and in fact the logic does not hold up well under careful analysis, as shown in Cummins and Weiss 1992b), it is not clear that it could equally be applied to public corporations. Such organizations presumably were more directly accountable to popularly elected representatives. Yet the same patterns evident in the American private market were found in tort jurisdictions with public automobile insurance systems. This point is illustrated in figure 3.2, which shows claims cost trends in Manitoba from 1985/86 through 1991/92. As shown in figure 3.2, Manitoba's public system saw a sharp rise in losses from bodily injury claims while property damage losses remained relatively stable (Manitoba Public Insurance Corporation 1993, 26; see also Kopstein, 1988, vol. 2, part 1).

Third, a key Profiteering Story claim about no-fault insurance rested on highly questionable statistical analysis. As emphasized previously, a good story accounts for a variety of different factual information. One of the potential attractions of the Profiteering Story was its ability to explain information that initially seemed to undermine the claims of no-fault advocates: the observed fact that insurance premiums were on average higher in no-fault jurisdictions. Such information was completely consistent with the Profiteering Story's problem diagnosis and policy prescription.

However, inferences drawn from the simple comparison of rates were valid only if there were strong grounds for believing that nothing simultaneously influenced the choice of insurance system and the level of premiums. That was not the case. The tort recovery system predated no-fault systems and remained the "default option." As shown earlier in this chapter, subnational governments tended to consider no-fault

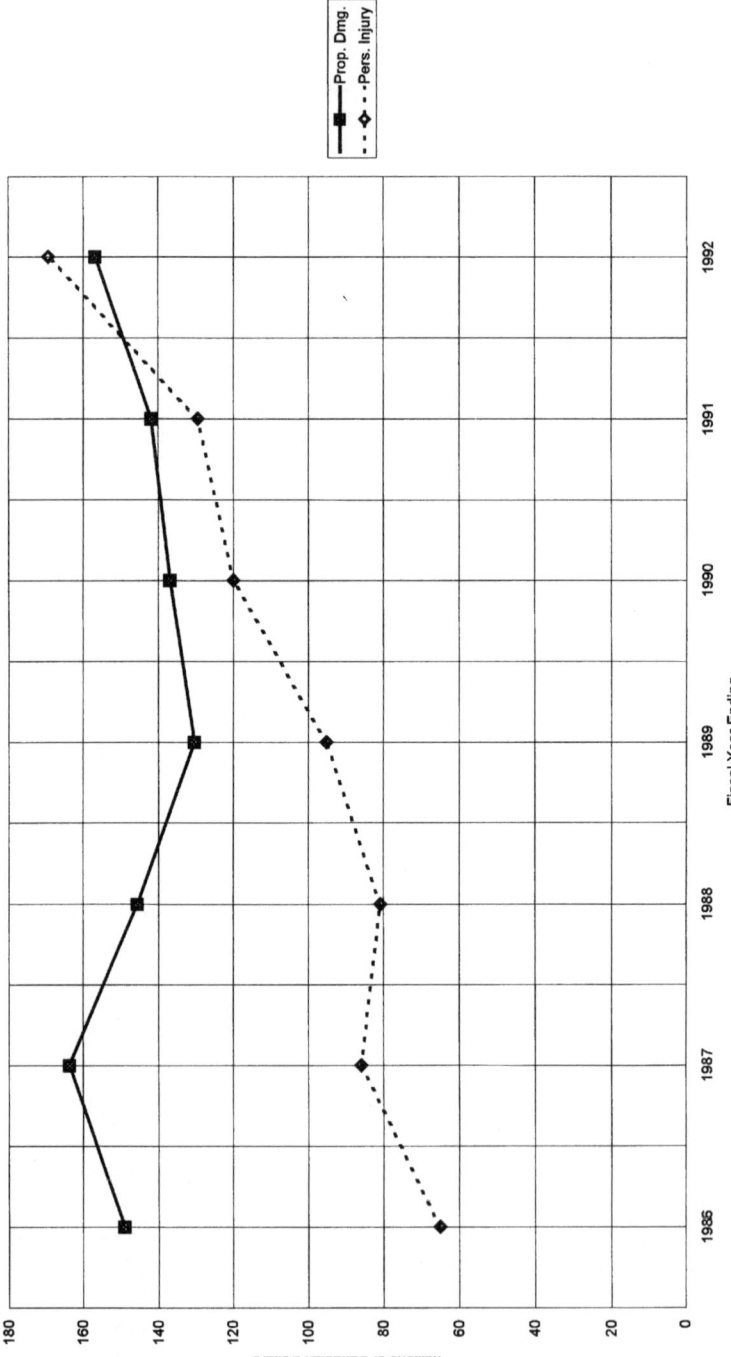

Figure 3.2. Claims Cost Trends in Manitoba, Fiscal Year 1985/86 through 1991/92
Source: MPIC 1993, 26.

only if they had a serious rates problem; automobile insurance was largely absent from the government agenda if premiums were relatively low and stable. Hence the finding of higher premiums in no-fault jurisdictions was likely spurious. In the more vivid metaphor of my colleague Michael Powers, judging it damning that rates were higher in no-fault jurisdictions was much the same as being surprised that many people under hospital care were very sick.

Fourth, as a group the policy experts tended to reject the premises of the Profiteering Story and accept the premises of the Pogo Story. Powers and I (1997) reached this conclusion based on an empirical study of the attitudes of that segment of the insurance policy community focused on the behavior of insurance markets. In table 3.1 I summarize responses to selected questions we posed to members of the

TABLE 3.1.
Selected Views of the Automobile Insurance Policy Community*

STATEMENT	Agree Strongly	Agree Somewhat	Disagree Somewhat	Disagree Strongly	Unsure
"Price collusion among insurance companies is prevalent."	3	8	14	68	7**
"Attorney involvement in automobile accident claims increases insurance loss costs."	79	13	3	2	2
"Reducing claims-related costs will lead to lower premiums."	58	36	2	1	4
"Regulator-imposed ceilings on insurance rates are likely to cause firms to restrict coverage and/or withdraw from the market."	70	27	2	1	1

*Data are taken from a survey of American Risk and Insurance Association (ARIA) members conducted by Edward Lascher and Michael Powers in the fall of 1995. A total of 405 ARIA members were surveyed, of whom 202 responded. For further information about this research, see Lascher and Powers 1997.
**Due to rounding, rows do not all sum to 100 percent.

American Risk and Insurance Association (ARIA).[14] As shown in table 3.1, ARIA members strongly rejected the notions that price collusion was prevalent among insurance companies, as the Profiteering Story suggested. At the same time ARIA members strongly agreed with the notion that attorney involvement in accident claims increased insurance loss costs, that reduction of claims costs would lead to lower premiums, and that regulator-imposed rate ceilings would cause constriction of the insurance market. All of these arguments were consistent with the Pogo Story.

I do not wish to claim that agreement with the above line of reasoning necessitated support for no-fault. One might sensibly have contended that 1) the Profiteering Story was implausible, and 2) the Pogo Story was generally accurate, but 3) no-fault was nevertheless an undesirable system. Some scholars have argued that adoption of no-fault encourages driver negligence. While this argument is controversial in the empirical literature, it may have formed the basis for opposition to no-fault unrelated to acceptance of one of the major stories.[15] However, since the Pogo Story was better supported by the facts than the Profiteering Story, policy prescriptions that were linked to the former should be viewed as having a stronger initial claim to likely success.

SUMMARY OF POLICY CHANGES

In the following chapters I give extensive attention to policy decisions in Pennsylvania, Rhode Island, and Ontario. To appreciate what these are "cases of," I return now to my classification of policy options.

Rate Freezes and Rollbacks

While several North American jurisdictions considered rate freezes and/or rollbacks during the period I studied, only a few actually adopted such options. Pennsylvania and Ontario were included in this group. In Pennsylvania mandatory rate reductions were tied to a more extensive reform package, including implementation of choice no-fault. In Ontario rate freezes were tried first and a strong no-fault system was tried later.

Tight Regulation

The Ontario government moved to tighten regulation at the same time as it attempted to control premiums through freezes/rollbacks. A few other jurisdictions tightened regulation as well, but most did not significantly alter their regulatory systems.

Conclusion

No-Fault Insurance

In chapter 7 I will consider in more depth the fate of no-fault throughout American and Canadian jurisdictions, since that topic is central to my analysis of the impact of institutional differences. For now, suffice it to indicate that only one American state either adopted any form of no-fault or moved to replace a weaker with a stronger no-fault law (e.g., replacing a monetary threshold system with a verbal threshold system). That state was Pennsylvania. No-fault proposals died in many state legislatures, including the Rhode Island General Assembly. In the meantime Ontario was one of three Canadian provinces that adopted strong no-fault proposals.

Public Automobile Insurance

No jurisdiction adopted a public automobile insurance system during the period I studied. Only Ontario seriously considered such a move. The battle over that proposal occurred after the above-mentioned policy changes were implemented in the province.

CONCLUSION

If the analysis in this chapter is accurate, automobile insurance reform decisions in large part turned on the extent to which politicians accepted one of two causal stories, only one of which (the Pogo Story) was well supported by the facts. In particular, adoption of no-fault required widespread acceptance of the Pogo Story. A crucial question is, therefore, what factors promoted or retarded story acceptance? I turn to that question in the following case study chapters.

NOTES TO CHAPTER 3

1. This is not to imply that the same product has the same value to different customers. For example, motorists in big cities who read constantly of property crimes in their areas may value the same dollar amount of comprehensive coverage more highly than people in farming communities who do not fear theft. For a thoughtful discussion of such issues, see England 1994.

2. Consider, for example, the case of Rhode Island. As I will discuss further in chapter 5, a large package of proposals aimed at reducing automobile insurance premiums was presented to the state legislature in 1993. However, the impact of most of these proposals was considered minor. Actual debate centered around two competing policy alternatives: legislation to adopt a verbal

threshold no-fault system and a bill to tighten regulation while imposing mandatory rate rollbacks.

3. While the first two approaches are related, they are not identical. A jurisdiction could move to more closely regulate providers without requiring rate freezes or rollbacks. On the other hand, if a jurisdiction was operating under a very loose regulatory regime, imposition of rate controls would simultaneously require tighter regulation, as occurred in Ontario in the mid-1980s.

4. In everyday conversation, the term "no-fault" is sometimes applied to systems that meet the first criterion (required first party benefits) but fail to meet the second criterion (restrictions on tort action). Thus by the late 1980s many American states and most Canadian provinces had adopted laws requiring that consumers purchase (and insurance providers offer) some amount of first party coverage for injuries sustained in automobile accidents. Rules of this sort are sometimes referred to as "add-on" no-fault laws, since the first party benefits simply supplement the recovery for injuries that can be obtained through the tort system. However, during the period of my study, add-on proposals did not surface as possible solutions to the problem of high insurance rates, undoubtedly because there was consensus that moving to an add-on system would not lead to lower premiums.

5. The literature advocating no-fault insurance is vast. For a particularly thorough analysis of how no-fault may work to lower costs, and the cost implications of different system design characteristics, see Carroll et al. 1991.

6. Source: interview with NDP party official.

7. The seminal work was Robert E. Keeton and O'Connell 1965. For a more recent discussion, see for example O'Connell 1989.

8. It should be noted that only trial attorneys taking plaintiffs' cases might be expected to oppose no-fault; insurance defense lawyers might not be expected to do so. Nevertheless, trial lawyer *organizations* have tended to oppose no-fault. For that reason I will use the more general term (trial attorneys) rather the more specific term (plaintiffs' attorneys).

9. The reference is to a famous line from Walt Kelly's "Pogo" cartoon strip. For an application of this line in another public policy context, see Wildavsky 1980, ch. 4.

10. Literature from a Pogo Story perspective often literally uses such language about "basic economics." See for example Berte 1991; Cheit and Youngwood 1991.

11. For a similar argument about the importance of avoiding relativism and evaluating the bases of conceptual systems, even while attempting to fully and fairly describe them, see Lakoff 1996, ch. 20.

12. For purposes of assessing the need to undertake antitrust action, the United States Department of Justice (DOJ) focuses on the level of industry concentration. Specifically, the DOJ uses a measure commonly known as the Herfindahl Index, which reflects the market shares of firms. A pure monopoly would have a score of 10,000 under this index. The national Herfindahl index for the automobile insurance market was 690 in 1989, indicating a relatively low degree of concentration in the industry (Cummins and Tennyson 1992, 98).

Even if the industry is competitive using conventional market concentration standards, many would argue that real-world competitiveness may be

Notes to Chapter 3

hampered by consumer problems in understanding and assessing insurance policies (see also Cheit and Youngwood 1991). In fact, in our 1995 survey 88 percent of ARIA respondents agreed strongly or agreed somewhat that "consumers have more difficulty evaluating differences in insurance policies than evaluating differences in most other products."

13. The following sources are among those supporting my conclusions regarding competitiveness and profitability in the automobile insurance industry, in both the United States and Canada: Cheit and Youngwood 1991; Cummins and Tennyson, 1992; Cummins and Weiss 1992b; Legislative Analyst 1990; Litzenberger and Nye 1987; Macey and Miller 1993; NAIC 1994; Osborne 1988; Standard & Poor's Corporation 1988; Sutton 1991.

14. A total of 405 ARIA members were surveyed, of whom 374 were Americans and 31 were Canadians.

15. For an argument that no-fault significantly increases driver negligence, see Devlin 1992. For a theoretical and empirical argument that the effects of no-fault are much more complex, see Cummins and Weiss 1992a.

4
Reform Enacted: Pennsylvania

"The [Pennsylvania] legislature is hopeless," says Herb Dennenberg, a former Pennsylvania insurance commissioner and an ardent backer of no-fault. "[Legislators] role over and play dead and let the trial lawyers take over."

—Quoted in Spiro and Mirvish (1989, 27)

[F]or the first time since I have been in the legislature dealing with auto insurance reform[...] we refrained from playing the old game of doing nothing unless the major special interest[s] agreed[....] I think particular tribute has to be paid[...] to this House, because it is this House that stood up on two occasions and put up the tough votes and refused to be seduced by the siren call of phony rate reductions without[...] cost savings. We did what all the smart money said was impossible to do.

—Pennsylvania State Representative Stephen Freind, during 1990 floor debate on final approval of an auto insurance reform package (Commonwealth of Pennsylvania 1990, 203–04)[1]

The Pennsylvania case demands attention because the decision to embrace even a limited form of no-fault differs from the customary pattern. When then Governor Robert P. Casey signed into law "Act 6" on 7 February 1990, which included provisions for a choice no-fault system, it represented the first time that a traditional tort state had adopted any sort of no-fault system since the middle of the 1970s.[2] Furthermore, while no-fault legislation made progress in some state legislatures between 1990 and 1995, no state actually moved away from the traditional tort system.

Yet the significance of Act 6 goes beyond the no-fault provisions. The Pennsylvania measure was probably the most comprehensive automobile insurance reform package of any type enacted by an American state legislature in recent years. Along with the changes to the tort system, Act 6 imposed mandatory rate reductions and established a medical cost containment system. To achieve these ends losses were imposed on three major groups, all of which opposed the legislation, and all of which were considered highly influential in Pennsylvania (Crotty 1993; Thomas 1993). The trial attorneys were losers in that Act 6 partially eroded the unlimited right to sue for damages that trial attorney associations everywhere stoutly defend. The insurance companies—commonly backers of no-fault in other circumstances—were left with required rate cuts that they had fought. Medical providers experienced undesired changes to the reimbursement system for services to automobile accident victims.

Why did Pennsylvania lawmakers enact the legislation that became Act 6? Why did they defeat alternative reform measures that promised significant premium savings without imposing as wide-ranging losses on powerful interest groups? In this chapter I focus on such questions. I argue that there is strong reason to believe that Pennsylvania legislators were convinced that the approach contained in Act 6 would work, while other approaches were doomed to failure. Furthermore, such judgments were based on widespread acceptance of the Pogo Story (see chapter 3) by the end of 1989.

CONTEXT

Before turning to the automobile insurance issue, two features of Pennsylvania's political environment are especially notable. First, the 1989–90 Pennsylvania General Assembly was among the most professionalized of American state legislatures, according to various indices.[3] This meant that lawmakers were paid sufficiently to devote their full attention to legislative duties, that the General Assembly itself met regularly throughout the year, and that lawmakers were provided significant staff support. Second, Pennsylvania was a politically competitive state. Control of the legislature and governorship regularly alternated between the two political parties (Doukas 1989, 28). Such competitiveness was evident in 1989–90. Governor Casey was a Democrat, having succeeded a Republican. The Republicans controlled the State Senate by a thin margin, with 27 of 50 seats. The Democrats narrowly controlled the House of Representatives, with 104 of 203 seats.

With respect to the automobile insurance issue, the most important thing to note is that the late 1980s was a period of widespread concern about rates, especially in metropolitan Philadelphia. Indeed, it was common to term the rates problem a "crisis" (see for example Powers 1989). Perceptions that Pennsylvania motorists faced a particularly large burden in obtaining insurance accorded with available data. In 1989 average total automobile insurance expenditures for consumers in that state ranked tenth highest among the fifty states and the District of Columbia, while average expenditures for the liability coverage alone ranked sixth highest (National Association of Insurance Commissioners 1993, 9). One study of data from the late 1980s indicated that premiums in Philadelphia were the highest among twenty-seven local urban markets (Smith and Wright 1992). Rates also had been rising rapidly; during the six years before the reform battle I studied, insurance rates had escalated at more than three times the rate of increase in the Consumer Price Index (Powers 1989).

Automobile insurance reform was not a new topic for the Pennsylvania General Assembly in 1989–90. Like most states, Pennsylvania required that motorists carry automobile insurance, making it especially difficult for lawmakers to avoid responsibility for public concerns. In fact, the legislature had moved in different directions in response to such concerns. The state had adopted a weak no-fault law in 1974 (the law was weak in the sense that it placed only mild restrictions on tort action, while providing generous "first party" benefits to accident victims regardless of fault status). According to several studies, the combination of a low threshold and generous first party benefits led to a proliferation of lawsuits and rapidly escalating costs (Duggan 1994; Harley 1989). In 1984 the restrictions on tort actions were repealed and required first party benefits were lowered.

Within the General Assembly, there was a widespread belief that the 1984 law had failed to address the general public's desire for lower rates, although it may have served the needs of various interest groups.[4] This sentiment was evident in some of the legislative debate that culminated in Act 6. Following are illustrative statements made during discussion of the final conference committee report; the statements are from a proponent and opponent, respectively.[5]

> Now, I was not here in 1984 when the automobile insurance law was changed [. . .] in this legislature, but it appeared to me through my research on this bill and reading the legislative record that in the past when so-called reforms were passed, [the] people who gained were the people who participated in the [legislative] system and not those for whom the system was created to benefit—[those] being the policyholder[s].
>
> [The proponent of the conference report] admits he was not here in the early [1980s], but many of us were, and the debate was around the same sort of question—whether we are going to be able to guarantee a rate reduction or not. We know what happened. [The rate reduction] did not come about.

THE BATTLE OVER INSURANCE REFORM
Proposals and Partisans

The legislation that came to be Act 6 was introduced at the bequest of the governor in the spring of 1989 and was in a very real sense a Casey administration bill. The appointed insurance commissioner and her Insurance Department, in coordination with the governor's office, developed many of the specific proposals contained in the legislation (albeit, often cribbing from other reform plans).[6] Administration representatives also put together a strategy for securing passage of the measure, produced specific information to provide legislators, worked with the media to obtain favorable press coverage, and actually engaged in extensive lobbying of lawmakers. When the legislation stalled at the end of 1989, administration officials engaged in personal negotiations to revive it. Casey himself made the issue a personal priority, considering it "without a doubt the biggest consumer issue in the State." By all accounts, he was actively involved in attempting to secure passage of the reform legislation.[7]

The administration's plan was explicitly intended to "stop the skyrocketing cost of auto insurance in [Pennsylvania] once and for all."[8] While retaining mandatory first party coverage, the plan required that consumers be offered the opportunity to choose a lower cost "limited tort" (i.e., no-fault) plan.[9] People covered by such policies could sue for pain and suffering only if they sustained serious injuries, as defined by law. In other words, a verbal threshold was to be used. Additionally, the bill aimed to institute a system of medical cost containment for treatment of automobile accident victims. Among other things, the bill generally limited reimbursement of medical providers to 110 percent of reimbursement that would be provided for similar services under the federal Medicare program. The bill also contained "pro-consumer" provisions relating to insurance fraud, cancellation of insurance policies, and other matters. Last but not least important, the administration's plans included mandatory rate cuts for specific types of coverage tied to projected cost reductions under the legislation. It was claimed that all consumers would receive some savings; those choosing the limited tort option would receive significantly greater savings.

The governor's plan drew both on other cost control ideas that had been circulating and on the lessons administration officials had learned from earlier failed efforts to achieve auto insurance reform. Casey previously had advocated adoption of a mandatory verbal threshold no-fault system, but implementing legislation was still-born in the General Assembly. Administration officials acknowledged they had insufficient legislative support to obtain enactment of a mandatory no-fault bill. As a fall-back they turned to a choice proposal similar to one that had earlier been offered by Representative Stephen Freind. Interestingly, as the administration itself acknowledged, the idea for a medical cost control plan was taken from representatives of the Pennsylvania Trial Lawyers Association (PTLA), which had first proposed such a plan.

Within the General Assembly, the administration plan received strong support from some individual legislators, especially in the House of Representatives. Two lawmakers played an especially large role in leading the battle for legislative enactment. One was Representative Freind, a conservative Republican who nevertheless made common cause with the Democratic administration on this issue. In fact, the implementing legislation was sometimes referred to as the "Freind/Casey" bill. The other was Representative Richard Hayden, a relatively junior Democratic legislator. Freind and Hayden took the lead in defending the plan during legislative debate and in attempting to ward off alternative proposals. Interestingly, both Hayden and Freind were attorneys. However, both indicated that they believed that an explosion of litigation was largely responsible for escalating insurance premiums in Pennsylvania.

Casey's plan also received some support in the mass media. The state's largest circulation newspaper, the *Philadelphia Inquirer*, provided backing that both administration officials and some opponents considered important (and not coincidentally, the administration cultivated such support). The *Inquirer* provided continuous, often front-page, coverage of the battle over insurance reform. Furthermore, the newspaper consistently editorialized in favor of the Casey proposal and against legislative efforts to undermine it. At one point the newspaper went so far as to subtitle an editorial (1989b) on an impending Senate vote as follows: "The forces of evil confront the forces of good in the Pa. Senate today—who will win?" The *Inquirer* also printed stories that were potentially embarrassing to lawmakers. These included articles about campaign contributions to individual legislators by interest groups opposed to the Casey plan and about the perquisite that allowed lawmakers to obtain state fund reimbursement for their own automobile insurance expenses (Cohn and Fish 1989; Cohn, Fish, and Enda 1989).

The Casey administration and its allies faced opposition from some individual legislators holding influential positions. In particular, the chairman of the Senate Banking and Insurance Commission opposed the Casey proposal and supported his own insurance reform plan. Among other things, the legislation backed by the chairman called

The Battle Over Insurance Reform   57

for reductions in mandatory coverage and restrictions on insurance companies' ability to cancel policies. In a lengthy exchange of correspondence, the chairman repeatedly argued that this plan would provide meaningful savings to consumers, while the insurance commissioner challenged this claim.

By the time the Casey plan reached the General Assembly, a number of other insurance reform proposals had been offered by individual legislators. Not all such plans were strictly inconsistent with the governor's proposal, but they represented different ways of attempting to achieve premium reductions. Much of the legislation focused on problems of insurance affordability and availability in greater Philadelphia. For example, one plan called for setting up a state operated, "single provider" system for insuring Philadelphia residents, presumably at a lower cost.

Both the PTLA and the Insurance Federation of Pennsylvania (IFP), a trade association for the insurance companies, actively opposed the Casey plan, if for different reasons. As a PTLA representative indicated to me, the trial lawyers were "philosophically opposed to no-fault," believing that the tort system worked better. While the trial lawyers viewed a choice system as less objectionable than a mandatory plan, they remained opposed. The IFP meantime supported a required no-fault plan, but objected to the Casey plan which combined a choice no-fault plan with mandatory premium reductions (see Laskow 1990). As an IFP representative acknowledged to me, the industry was worried about the short-term negative impact of rate cuts without seeing potential long-term benefits for industry health.

Various medical provider groups eventually expressed opposition to the medical cost control provisions of the Casey bill, and some even sued to prevent implementation after the measure was signed into law. However, groups such as the Pennsylvania Medical Society were not actively involved in the legislative battle until the bill was close to final approval.[10] The reasons for this are unclear. There was some speculation that their representatives failed to appreciate the significance and/or political feasibility of the reform proposals at earlier stages of the legislative process.

Arguments and Tactics

The Casey administration engaged in both an "inside" and an "outside" strategy to secure enactment of the insurance reform bill. The inside strategy focused especially on providing lawmakers with detailed information about how their constituents would benefit from the legislation.[11] The research arm of the Department of Insurance developed actuarial estimates of savings in various lines of coverage from implementing bill provisions. Drawing on regional cost data, the department was then able to estimate savings for specific legislative constituencies. The department provided individual lawmakers with packets containing such information.

Administration officials also conducted extensive efforts to "educate" the news media about automobile insurance reform. Department of Insurance officials held many one-on-one meetings with reporters to explain the rationale for the Casey plan and to argue for its superiority to other proposals. Top department officials made themselves available to answer press questions. Press releases were commonly provided.

The governor himself both lobbied individual legislators and appealed directly to the general public. To the legislators Casey repeatedly stressed that his plan was not "phony," but based on real cost savings resulting from lowering medical costs and reducing litigation. According to Casey this emphasis was important especially given the past failure of reform efforts; "to be willing to sign on," legislators had to be convinced that the proposal would actually deliver on the promise of lowering rates. In public press conferences and similar forums, Casey stressed the "special interest" angle. He portrayed the battle as one between consumers and the "special interests" opposing his plan.[12]

Interestingly, the administration and its allies deliberately drew a distinction between their plan and the rate reduction scheme called for under California's Proposition 103. The California measure had received national publicity. It was widely known that Proposition 103 was tied up in the courts, and the rate rollbacks had not yet materialized.[13] Backers of the Casey plan argued that with its cost reduction features, their plan would succeed where the California plan had not.

It appears that the organized opposition to the Casey plan, led by the insurance industry and trial lawyers, concentrated on an inside strategy. That is, they attempted to take their case directly to lawmakers, rather than influence legislators indirectly through instigating grassroots pressure.[14] During informal meetings with legislators, PTLA representatives pressed for consideration of alternative means of reducing premiums. The trial lawyers also argued against the merits of no-fault, contending that the tort system served as a more effective deterrent to bad driving and that as a matter of justice those responsible for causing accidents should pay for damages. Insurance industry representatives pushed for mandatory no-fault, claiming it would lead to greater premium reductions. The industry also raised concerns about the savings projected under the Casey plan.

The Battle Over Insurance Reform

Legislative Action

Governor Casey announced his plan on 6 June 1989. The administration then held discussions with lawmakers about the proposal. The actual implementing language first appeared in legislative form on 13 June as amendments offered by Representative Hayden to a bill already on the House floor. There followed extensive debate on the proposal.

Handing the administration a victory of sorts, the House passed a version of the Casey plan. The House first agreed to an amendment requiring a minimum 25 percent reduction on all insurance rates. Hayden and Freind strenuously objected to this change, arguing that the 25 percent figure was arbitrary and not supported by corresponding cost reductions; the administration shared such opposition.[15] However, the legislators found the change sufficiently appealing to adopt it by a vote of 125 to 75. The statement of one representative immediately before the vote is revealing about the nature of this appeal.

> Today we are here for one reason: to answer the complaints of our constituents about the high cost and the unavailability of auto insurance.... [The] amendment today of a rate cut is the only guarantee we have in writing that we can take back to our constituents and say[:] here is a rate reduction of 25 percent in your insurance.[16]

Nevertheless the House action was viewed by some as a partial success for the Casey administration, since the chamber had given its approval to a measure containing the tort restriction opposed by the trial attorneys and rate reductions opposed by insurance companies (*Philadelphia Inquirer* 1989a).

Initially the Senate dealt with the Casey plan more harshly. The Senate Business and Insurance Committee voted against the proposal and instead approved the plan by its chairman, who claimed his bill would slash rates by as much as 45 percent. Casey attacked the measure as "worthless" and "meaningless." The governor reiterated his belief in the necessity of limiting medical expenses and reducing lawsuits. The *Inquirer* also slammed the committee's action, arguing senators had "flinched" in facing a "crucial test of will on lowering auto insurance costs." Nevertheless, in a defeat for the governor, the full Senate also voted against the Casey plan on 28 June, defeating it by a margin of 30 to 17. The Senate subsequently approved the Business and Insurance Committee chairman's plan and adjourned for a summer recess (Enda 1989a, 1989b, 1989c, 1989d, 1989e).

No legislative action was taken between the summer recess and December of 1989. However, behind-the-scenes negotiations between legislative leaders and various interested parties (though apparently not the Casey administration) produced a "compromise plan" that was sent to a joint House-Senate conference committee. The legislation included a medical cost control plan similar to the one sought by Casey and his allies, but not the optional no-fault provisions. The bill also included a mandatory across-the-board 10 percent premium cut for all motorists, an additional 20 percent reduction for "safe drivers" (as defined in the legislation), and still further cuts for motorists in specified circumstances (e.g., those driving cars with air bags). According to proponents, the legislation would result in overall premium reductions of up to 50 percent. The "compromise plan" had the support of the PTLA; insurance company representatives expressed concern about the mandatory rate rollbacks. Casey and his legislative allies expressed strong opposition. Yet on 11 December the Senate approved the plan by a vote of 32 to 16 (Enda 1989f, 1989g).

It was at this point that the most dramatic event in the saga of the Pennsylvania reform legislation occurred. On 12 December the conference report was taken up by the full House, with ratification from that forum representing the last barrier to a bill reaching the governor's desk. The majority leader, a Democrat, presented the report and urged its adoption, stressing the consumer savings that he said would result. Yet in an action widely seen as unexpected, the rank-and-file membership rejected the plan by a vote of 120 to 80, making it highly possible that no reform plan would be approved by the General Assembly during the legislative session.[17]

The vote in the House was preceded by lengthy, strenuous debate which by various accounts moved several legislators to vote against the conference report.[18] Opponents hammered at the theme of avoiding "phony reform." Representative Hayden spoke first, and set the tone:

> Since brevity is the order of the evening, I will get right to the point here. I would ask you to vote "no" on this conference report for the very simple reason that this proposal is not going to work. If you look at this proposal, you will see that there is a 10-percent across-the-board discount for everybody and a 20-percent discount for safe drivers. This is over and above other reductions which are in the bill[. . . .] [W]hen I finished adding up what these supposed discounts were going to be for [an individual taking all deductions], I found out that the insurance company is going to have to pay [that individual] to have insurance. Now, this is Christmas and we are all in the Christmas spirit, and I would certainly like insurance companies to pay for everybody's insurance, but if you believe that those discounts are ever going to take place you are sadly mistaken[.]

Subsequent speakers echoed many of the same themes.

The Battle Over Insurance Reform

[...] Mr. Speaker, I hold out to you that this bill is automobile insurance fraud. I think it has been explained to all of you that until we stop the proliferation of lawsuits, we cannot do anything about insurance rates[.]
[...] I think we all agree on several things. Number one, probably the greatest crisis facing our constituents is ever rising auto insurance rates, and number two, we have to provide meaningful auto insurance reform which has mandated reductions, but I think the key word is "meaningful." What we did before in this House was meaningful. We recognized the fact that you cannot by definition have auto insurance reform unless and until you attack the two major [reasons] for rates going up: first and most importantly the proliferation of lawsuits, and secondly, rising health care costs[....] There is no such thing, Mr. Speaker, as a free lunch in this world. [In the conference committee proposal] we have these mystical mandated reductions, but there is nothing whatsoever in the bill in cost savings to justify the rate reductions[....] I think the major theme song for this legislation, if it is passed, is "California Here We Come."
[...] I have no problem with mandating a rate reduction if the bill that we are considering allows the insurance companies to effect some of these reductions, but this legislation does nothing like that. If you look over it, you will find that about 30 percent of all the provisions that we are considering tonight are provisions that increase the costs to the insurance companies[....] [The bill requires] a whole list of things that the insurance industry is supposed to do at no additional cost in premium to our constituents, and yet, at the same time, we are asking [insurance companies] to in addition reduce rates by 20 percent. It just does not make sense.
I am opposing this conference report for three or four reasons. First of all, it seems to me that this is a report that promises what it cannot deliver[....] Now, let us look at this conference report and see if it is confiscatory. In fact, it is indeed a rollback unsupported by savings.[19]

After the collapse of the "compromise plan," representatives of the Casey administration and key legislators met in private sessions to craft another proposal. This time substantial progress was made toward a negotiated settlement. Agreement was reached by the end of January 1990. The new plan contained the main elements of Casey's original legislation, including provisions for a choice no-fault system and medical cost containment. There were also to be reductions in the amount of insurance coverage consumers were required to purchase, as others had advocated. Additionally, the plan included broader rate rollback provisions than the administration originally had desired. Nevertheless, negotiators jettisoned the 25 percent across-the-board cut contained in the bill that passed the House originally; Insurance Department officials contended that the agreed-to premium reductions were justified by actuarial projections of claims cost savings.[20] A second conference report on the implementing legislation was approved by both houses on 7 February and signed by Governor Casey later that day.

EXPLAINING LEGISLATIVE DECISIONS IN PENNSYLVANIA

For the sake of clarity, I will divide my explanation of Pennsylvania's enactment of automobile insurance reform into two parts. In this section I will focus on Pennsylvania-specific factors that might have changed in such a way as to make it more probable that the General Assembly would have adopted the Casey plan. Until the end of chapter 4, I will refrain from providing a detailed comparison of Pennsylvania and other American states. The cross-sectional comparison will be more appropriate after I have discussed the case of Rhode Island, where reform efforts failed. There is no inconsistency between the longitudinal and cross-sectional perspectives; both underscore the importance of ideas.

If pressure theory sufficiently explained the change in policy direction in Pennsylvania, we would expect one or more of the following to have been true:

- During the crucial year of 1989 (or shortly before then), the positions of groups with respect to automobile insurance reform options should have changed in a manner favoring the Casey plan (e.g., groups previously opposing the proposal should have moved toward support).
- The amount of overt pressure coming from supporters should have increased and/or the amount of such pressure coming from opponents should have decreased.
- Changes should have occurred making legislative decisions with respect to the Casey plan more traceable (cf. Arnold 1990) for diffuse groups than such decisions were previously, and/or more traceable than other policy options.

These expectations were not met. Consider first the interest group alignment. If anything, the interest group alignment changed in a way that was unfavorable to the Casey plan, as traditional enemies (notably the trial lawyers and insurance companies) coalesced against the proposal, albeit for different reasons. Pennsylvania insurance companies had supported earlier no-fault plans, but opposed the version contained in Act 6. Nor was there any indication that pressure from any of these groups diminished over time, especially during the crucial 1989 battles. The insurance industry and trial attorneys also demonstrated willingness to invest considerable resources in fighting the Casey plan (Enda 1989e).

It is also difficult to make the argument that enactment of Act 6 can be attributed to decisions on automobile insurance reform becoming more traceable over time. Certainly consumers were angry in 1989 and were seen as likely to reward/punish lawmakers based on what happened to automobile insurance rates. Yet this was also true in earlier years, including 1988 when the first Casey plan failed. Nor had anything intrinsic to the automobile insurance issue changed that made it more probable that consumers would perceive a connection between legislative votes and real-world results.

Another troubling aspect of the pressure theory explanation is that it fails to provide guidance as to why lawmakers would have moved to back the Casey plan rather than other proposals. It would be one thing if the Casey plan had been the only one that could have been said to aid consumers as a group; a sophisticated pressure theorist (such as Arnold) might then have focused on activating the diffuse, inattentive public. But several of the proposals made such a claim, and some were alleged to provide significant premium savings without the tradeoffs necessitated by no-fault. In fact, some comments from individual Pennsylvania legislators make explicit the attractiveness of the alternative proposals. For example, one state representative indicated that she had supported the first conference committee report (containing what Casey and his allies called a phony rate reduction plan) because she found it "very difficult to go home and tell my constituents that I voted against the plan that mandated [rate] reductions."[21] Presumably other legislators had equivalent concerns about constituency views. Why did they not support the conference report? Pressure theory does not help us answer this question.

An alternative explanation is that "cues on the merits" increased in such a way as to make the Casey plan seem more likely to work. Consistent with the overall emphasis in this book, it might also be imagined that Pennsylvania lawmakers increasingly rejected the Profiteering Story, accepted the Pogo Story, and concluded that the Casey proposal matched well with the latter. I will argue that these expectations were met.

The most direct evidence for such a claim would be derived from a "before and after" survey of Pennsylvania lawmakers. Such evidence is lacking. Nevertheless, there are some indirect signs that a politics-of-ideas-type argument can help explain the change of policy direction in Pennsylvania. These signs are consistent with the expectations outlined in the last section of chapter 2. Such evidence includes the following:

- Governor Casey, his administration, and their supporters offered a consistent, coherent account of what was necessary to reduce rates. While such a line of argument may have been unfamiliar to many lawmakers at the start of the 1989–90 session, it was much harder for legislators to have been unaware of it by the end of 1989, when the argument had been repeated so often.
- The account offered by Casey and his allies was virtually an exact restatement of the Pogo Story outlined in chapter 3. That is, the Casey account held that spiraling legal and medical costs (rather than, say, uncommonly high profits or industry attempts to recoup for past investment losses) had caused the crisis in insurance rates. Consequently, only a plan that addressed those problems would work. The Casey plan was said to do so; others were said to fail that test.
- The move to oppose the Casey plan by all the major interest groups can be seen as a source cue that actually contributed to legislators becoming convinced that the proposal was on the right track. That is, the fact that all major groups were opposed helped to signal that the plan (a) was not the secret handiwork of one of the groups and (b) might actually aid the broad interests of constituents who were not lobbying in Harrisburg. As indicated, Casey and his allies attempted to exploit such a source cue.
- Potentially critical information consistent with the Casey argument/Pogo Story was presented at a key time during the 1989 debate. This information consisted of a series in the *Philadelphia Inquirer* emphasizing the importance of lawsuits and inflated medical costs for the state's high premiums (Fish and Cohn 1989).
- During 1989 the insurance commissioner and her Insurance Department provided legislators with very detailed, constituency-specific information about the impact of the proposal. The ability of the department to provide such information may well have provided a signal to lawmakers of the credibility of the administration's plan.
- The evolution of votes in the General Assembly, especially the House, was consistent with an explanation stressing learning about the merits of different policy proposals. In June of 1989 House members voted in favor of an across-the-board 25 percent cut; they voted against a similar proposal in December. This is what would be expected if lawmakers increasingly had come to accept the Pogo Story.
- Pennsylvania legislators tended to share a common perception: previous reform efforts had failed. This understanding would seem to have made them especially sensitive to making sure that they "got it right this time."

Epilogue: Did Act 6 Work?

Additionally, comments from lawmakers themselves indicate that, at least by the end of 1989, they generally had come to believe the problem diagnosis offered by the administration and its allies. I have already stressed the comments made during debate on the first conference report, emphasizing the difference between "real" and "phony" reform. Comments made during debate on the second conference report (approved in January 1990) suggest that by that time even opponents accepted the administration's premises. Ten state representatives and two senators spoke in favor of defeating the report. A few of the opponents complained that the no-fault provisions had been watered down too much to achieve real savings, and several expressed skepticism about whether the rate rollbacks would occur. None of the opponents, however, clearly challenged the notion that reducing lawsuits and lowering medical costs was necessary to lower premiums.

EPILOGUE: DID ACT 6 WORK?

A major theme of this book is the importance of legislators' judgments about the consequences of policies. A major theme of this chapter is that Pennsylvania lawmakers were likely to conclude that the proposal sponsored by the Casey administration would work. Given this emphasis, it is natural to attempt to determine whether such a judgment was accurate. After all, it is logically possible for lawmakers to reach a consensus about likely policy consequences that is in fact unwarranted. From a normative perspective, we should evaluate legislative learning more favorably if it produces judgments about policy consequences that are borne out by subsequent events.

What were the goals of Act 6? Again, according to all parties, including opponents of the measure, Act 6 was aimed at reducing insurance rates for motorists generally. Additionally, Casey and his allies explicitly indicated that their plan was designed not to be confiscatory, and thereby risk either being overturned by the courts or prompting insurance companies to withdraw coverage. This meant that if anything, Act 6 was supposed to result in an improved market for insurance companies by reducing the costs of doing business. Some opponents, notably representatives of the insurance industry, expressed skepticism about the cost reductions and argued that the measure would instead further weaken the market. Yet viewed in this manner the differences between the industry and the administration were reducible to varying predictions about legislative consequences—predictions that are subject to empirical test.

A first test of the success of Act 6 was implementation of its provisions. Experience in other states, notably California, showed that mandatory rate reductions unaccompanied by industry cost savings were often prohibited by the courts.[22] Predictably, after passage of the measure, various organizations filed lawsuits aimed at preventing provisions of Act 6 from taking effect. Insurance companies sued the Insurance Department in both federal and state court, seeking relief from the rate rollback provisions. Medical provider groups filed actions to overturn the medical cost containment provisions.

These efforts to block implementation were unsuccessful. Essentially the Insurance Department won the court battles, and the provisions of Act 6 were preserved virtually intact. Courts rejected such arguments as those by insurance companies that Act 6 represented an unconstitutional denial of a fair rate of return.[23] By the middle of 1990 the rollbacks began to take effect, and consumers were presented with the new set of coverage options, including the choice of limited tort.

Given implementation, the next issues to examine are whether Act 6 reduced premiums, lowered industry costs, and improved the market for automobile insurance. Sufficient time has passed to compare the experience in Pennsylvania before and after Act 6 and to compare Pennsylvania's experience with that of other states. In figures 4.1 through 4.4, I summarize a variety of data obtained from the National Association of Insurance Commissioners (1993, 1994) relevant to these issues.

In a nutshell, the data contained in the following figures are consistent with a highly favorable evaluation of Act 6. The data suggest that Act 6 indeed led to significant premium reductions and lower costs, without harming industry profitability. Figure 4.1 shows the trend in average automobile insurance expenditures for consumers in Pennsylvania and the nation as a whole. As can be seen, Pennsylvania's expenditures were relatively high before 1990, but fell after enactment of Act 6 and since that time have been close to the national average. Figure 4.2 shows the trend in combined insurance premiums (i.e., average liability premiums plus average collision premiums plus average comprehensive premiums), which is another measure of the costliness of insurance for consumers.[24] These data are also consistent with the conclusion that Act 6 was successful. Figure 4.3 shows that claims costs also have fallen dramatically since enactment of Act 6. Whereas before the legislation companies were facing about $90 in bodily injury losses for each $100 in liability premiums, after Act 6 that figure fell to about $80. Finally, figure 4.4 indicates that auto insurance profits (which actually were negative in 1989) have grown in both absolute and relative terms since enactment of Act 6.

Some other sources have also found that Act 6 has been successful. Notably, the Legislative Budget and Finance Committee (1993) reviewed the effects of the medical cost containment provisions of the

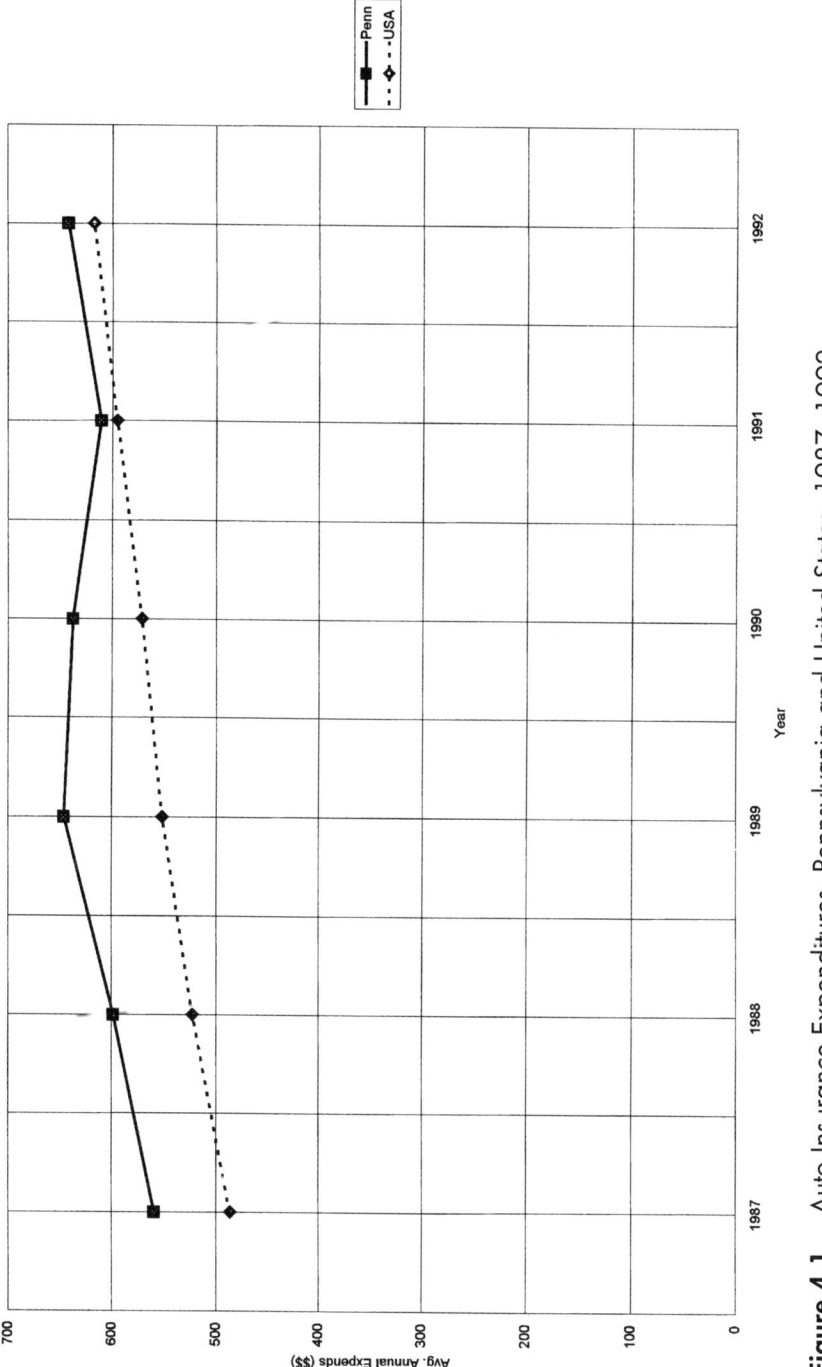

Figure 4.1. Auto Insurance Expenditures, Pennsylvania and United States, 1987–1992
Source: National Association of Insurance Commissioners (1993, 1994)

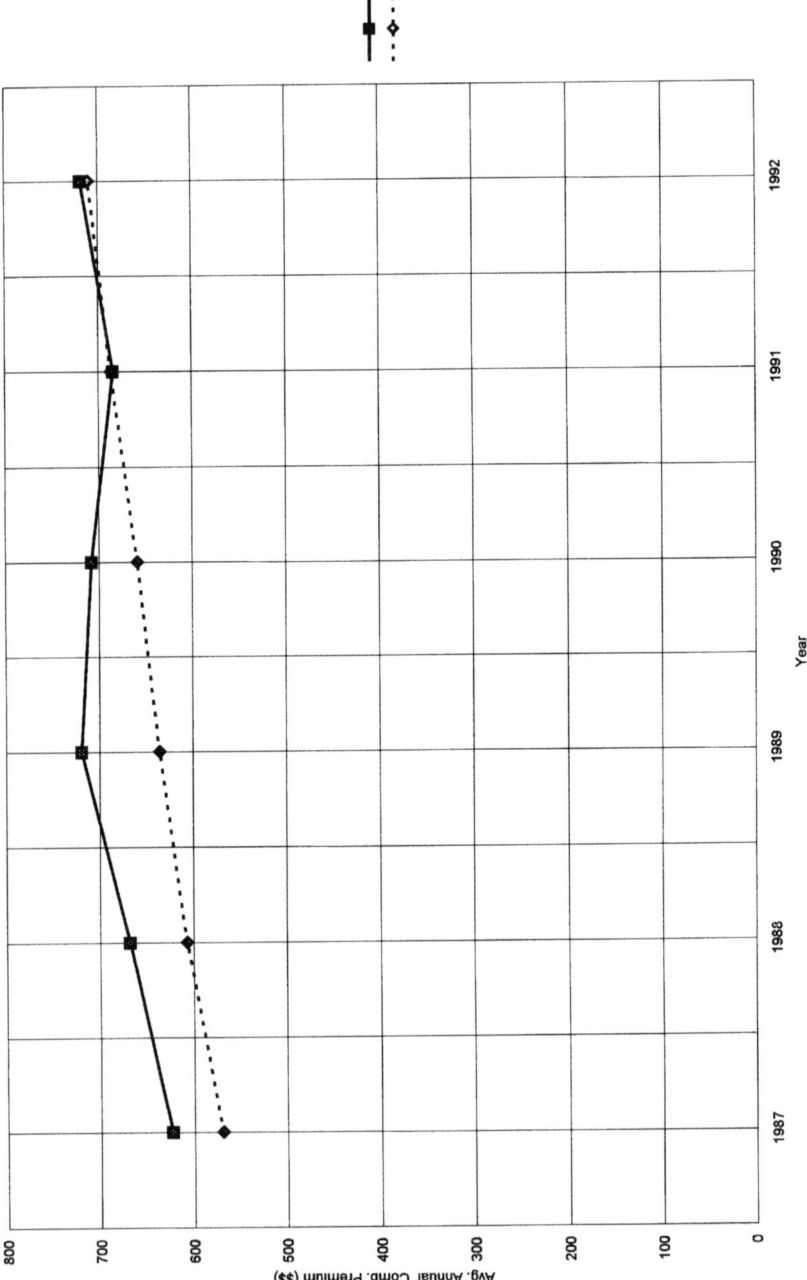

Figure 4.2. Combined Premiums, Pennsylvania and United States, 1987–1992
Source: National Association of Insurance Commissioners (1993, 1994)

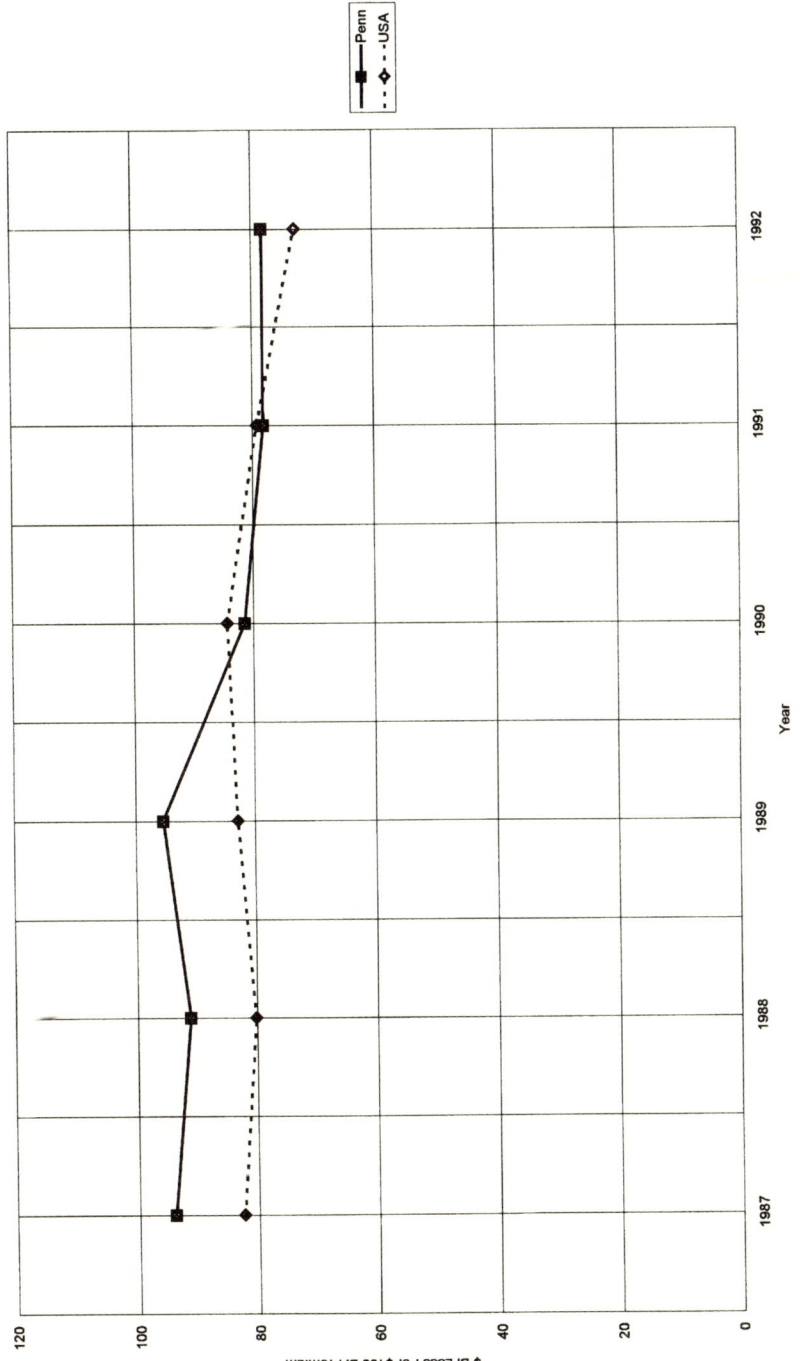

Figure 4.3. Loss Ratios, Pennsylvania and United States, 1987–1992
Source: National Association of Insurance Commissioners (1993, 1994)

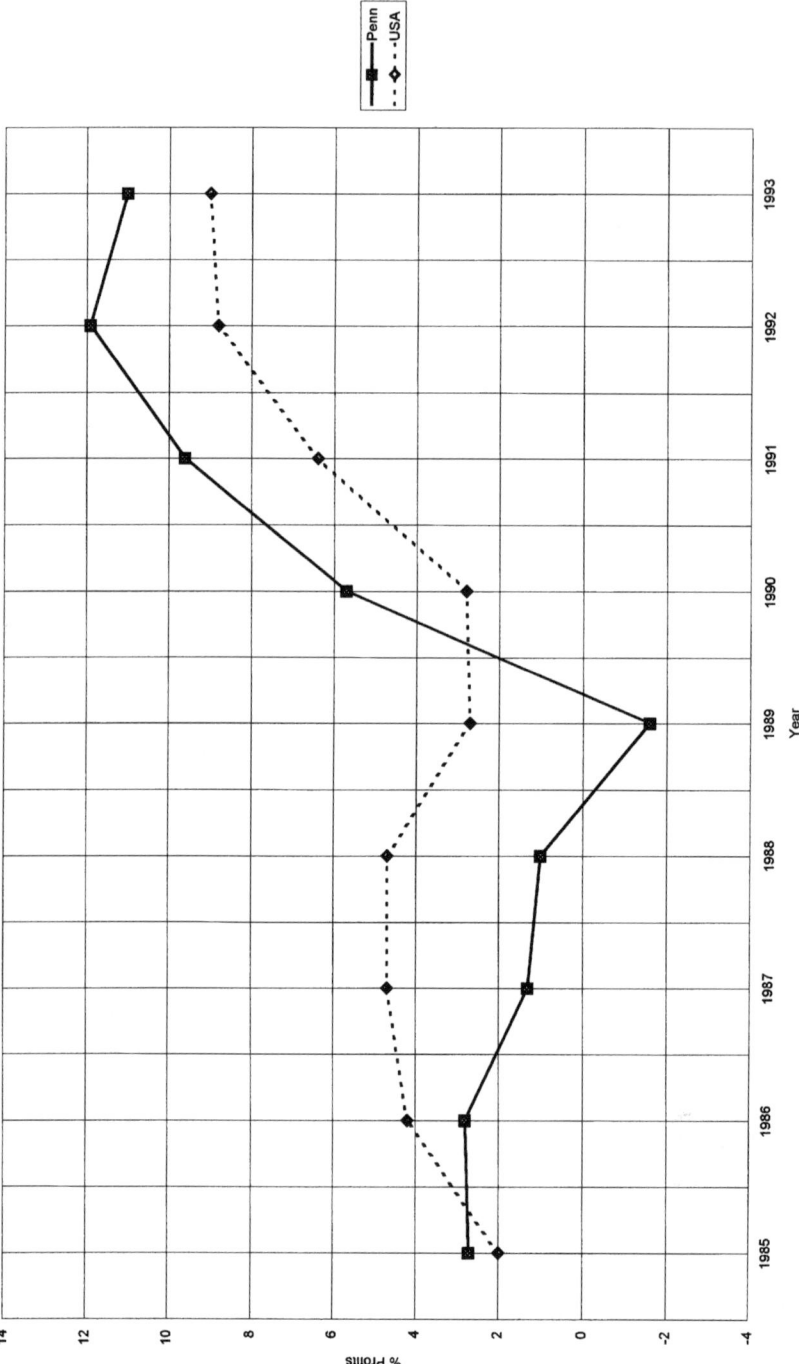

Figure 4.4. Auto Insurance Profits, Pennsylvania and United States, 1985–1993
Source: National Association of Insurance Commissioners (1993, 1994)

legislation. The committee found that Act 6 had "been helpful in controlling auto insurance rates." Even representatives of the Insurance Federation of Pennsylvania later gave Act 6 credit for helping to lower insurance costs.[25] Interestingly, it appears that the medical provisions, and not the no-fault provisions, provided most of the claims savings. This was due in part to the fact that subsequent to enactment of Act 6, most consumers retained full-tort coverage. No doubt this tendency was due in part to full tort being the default option and to an aggressive trial lawyers campaign to have consumers retain tort rights.

A complete evaluation of the success of Act 6 would give consideration to possible adverse consequences not anticipated by proponents.[26] It is beyond my capacity to consider such adverse consequences in-depth. Nevertheless, two points are worth noting. First, the Budget and Finance Committee report found no evidence that enactment of Act 6 seriously affected the availability of medical care to injured motorists. Second, the particular form of no-fault adopted in Pennsylvania would seem best designed to avoid creating perverse incentives for risky driving practices (because mandatory first party benefits were set relatively low, and access to such benefits was not affected by motorists' choices between the full-tort and limited-tort options).[27]

In short, Act 6 appears to have been successful in both the political and policy senses of the word. That is, the measure represented an instance in which major systematic changes were achieved despite fierce interest group opposition. As important, the real-world results appear consistent with the claims made by the act's sponsors.

NOTES TO CHAPTER 4

1. It should be noted that statements in the *Legislative Journal* are printed verbatim. Unlike the *Congressional Record*, the *Journal* includes neither statements made outside of floor sessions nor ex–post-facto "corrections" to legislators' arguments.

2. The Pennsylvania legislation is commonly referred to as "Act 6" because it was the sixth piece of legislation to receive final approval during the 1990 session of the General Assembly.

Following the middle of the 1970s, a few states strengthened existing no-fault laws by replacing monetary threshold with verbal threshold systems (e.g., New York), or by increasing the level of the monetary threshold (e.g., Massachusetts). For a summary of such changes, see Joost 1992.

3. See Mooney 1994. In 1989 Pennsylvania legislators received an annual salary of $47,000. They were also provided funds for legislative and district office operations. Furthermore, General Assembly sessions had been virtually year-long since the middle of the 1960s. For further detailed information about the General Assembly, see Doukas 1989.

4. Several nonlegislators I interviewed, including the governor himself, made similar arguments with respect to the 1984 legislation. See also Powers 1989.

5. Source: statements by Representatives Richard Hayden and Samuel Hayes, respectively, Commonwealth of Pennsylvania 1990, 225, 226.

6. In Pennsylvania and most other states, the insurance commissioner is appointed by the governor; in some states (e.g., California) the insurance commissioner is elected. During the period covered in this chapter, the Pennsylvania insurance commissioner was attorney Constance B. Foster.

7. Governor Casey himself claimed as much in a personal interview with the author on 13 September 1994.

8. Governor's office news release, 6 June 1989.

9. In a sense it is a misnomer to call the limited tort choice of the Casey plan a "no-fault" option, because the required first party benefits were to be the same for all people with insurance. Hence some degree of protection against accident losses was to be provided all insurance consumers, even those choosing a "traditional tort" plan. Nevertheless, the limited choice option shared a fundamental characteristic of all no-fault plans: lawsuits for recovery of accident damages were to be barred under some circumstances.

10. Several of those I interviewed emphasized the medical groups' lack of involvement. See also statements by Representative Steven Freind in Commonwealth of Pennsylvania 1990, 224; *Philadelphia Inquirer* 1990.

11. Interviews with people serving in the Department of Insurance in 1989–1990.

12. Interview with Governor Casey. The governor's account of the points he emphasized is consistent with newspaper stories; see for example Enda 1989g.

13. See for example the legislative debate contained in Commonwealth of Pennsylvania 1989b.

14. For example, I uncovered no evidence of efforts to use newspaper advertisements to raise concerns about legislation, as occurred in both Rhode Island and Ontario.

15. Even prior to the amendments, the administration-backed plan (contained in the Hayden proposal) contained language requiring specific percentage cuts in particular portions of insurance rates (e.g., coverage for bodily injury liability). However, the administration and its allies claimed the mandatory rate cuts were based on estimated cost reductions from the various provisions of the package. Furthermore, while all consumers were supposed to receive savings under the proposal, those electing the limited-tort option were supposed to receive a significantly greater amount.

16. Statement of Representative Edward Lucyk, Commonwealth of Pennsylvania 1989a, 993.

17. Both those I interviewed and newspaper accounts stressed that defeat of the conference plan was unexpected. See especially Enda 1989h.

18. Personal interviews. See also Enda 1989i.

19. Statements of Representatives Richard Hayden, James Gallen, Steven Freind, Harold Mowery, and David Wright, respectively, Commonwealth of Pennsylvania 1989b, 2142–47.

Notes to Chapter 4

20. The proposal also included a provision that made selection of full-tort coverage the "default" option under the choice no-fault system. This was an important decision because many consumers could be expected simply to take the default option, or be left with that option by virtue of failing to make a proper selection on insurance forms. A representative indicated to me that the default provision was a major victory for the trial lawyers. It is not clear, however, that the default provision was included to lessen the opposition of the trial lawyers. Instead, Casey and his allies may have come to believe that making full tort the default option was more defensible in the likely event of a court challenge to the choice no-fault system. Casey received advice to this effect from his staff.

21. Representative Kathrynann Durham, quoted in Enda 1989h.

22. In November of 1988, California voters passed Proposition 103, which aimed to reduce insurance rates through a mandatory 20 percent rollback. Following an insurance company suit, the California Supreme Court rejected such an across-the-board cut, and the measure was tied up in the courts for years. Five years after passage, major provisions of Proposition 103 had not been implemented; see Blau 1993. As noted, Governor Casey, state legislators, and others explicitly referred to the California experience during debate over automobile insurance reform in Pennsylvania.

23. See for example *Ohio Casualty Insurance v. Insurance Department of the Commonwealth of Pennsylvania*, 584 Atlantic 2d 1160 (Commonwealth of Pennsylvania, 1991).

24. In making comparisons across jurisdictions, the combined premium figures may be most appropriate, since consumers in different places may differ in their propensity to purchase particular types of coverage.

25. Motley 1993. However, one representative I interviewed contended that savings would have been much lower were it not for aggressive and successful IFP lobbying to create Insurance Department implementing regulations.

26. I am grateful to Joseph Bessette for emphasizing this point in commenting upon an earlier draft of this chapter.

27. The possibility of such perverse incentives stands as perhaps the most common criticism of no-fault plans among insurance economists; see especially Devlin 1992.

5
Reform Stymied: Rhode Island

> Policy-making may be shaped by ideas about the public interest, but they may not be *good* ideas.
> —Paul J. Quirk (1990, 199; emphasis in original)

The dramatic success of Act 6 in Pennsylvania should not obscure the central fact stressed earlier: in the United States, most recent, comprehensive efforts to reform automobile insurance laws have failed in state legislatures. If we are to truly understand decision making in this policy area, it is essential to examine in depth an instance of such failure and make comparisons to events in Pennsylvania. I pursue such tasks in this chapter.

My focus is on the Rhode Island General Assembly's failure to enact a no-fault bill in 1993, although I give some attention to earlier efforts to secure passage of similar legislation. For a number of reasons the comparison between the 1993 battle in Rhode Island and the earlier conflict in Pennsylvania is especially appropriate. In both cases the mass public was enraged by relatively high and quickly rising premiums. Not coincidentally, the issue was high on the agenda for state legislators. In both states the executive branch supported a reform package, at the heart of which was a no-fault proposal. Even the type of no-fault plan was similar. The legislation that became Act 6 contained provisions for a "choice" no-fault system with a verbal threshold; the Rhode Island bill also called for establishing such a system.[1] Interest-group activity was also high in both states.

Nonetheless, the legislative results differed, thereby providing an opportunity to assess possible explanatory factors that may or may not have varied across the two states. It is important not to overstate the difference in legislative decisions. As shown in chapter 4, passage of the Casey package was never a foregone conclusion, and as late as December of 1989 it appeared the legislation might be dead. Meantime, in 1993 Rhode Island lawmakers got closer to passing no-fault than they had in earlier years and closer than did legislators in most other states considering such a plan. Yet in the end Pennsylvania had a major new law and Rhode Island did not. The guiding question for this chapter is why this was so. Not surprisingly, I will argue that a significant part of the explanation pertains to differences in beliefs about reform's likely success.

CONTEXT

The 1993 battle over automobile insurance reform took place within a lawmaking body that was atypical of modern American legislatures. The Rhode Island General Assembly was an "old style" legislature, ranking low in terms of measures of professionalism (Mooney 1994). At the time the state's constitution (subsequently amended) limited legislative salaries to a maximum of $300 annually, making Rhode Island state lawmakers among the most poorly paid state legislators in the country. The conventional wisdom was that decisions were dominated by a few key leaders who were, at best, autocratic and at worst corrupt. Rank-and-file lawmakers traditionally had trouble even obtaining hearings on legislation not supported by leaders.[2]

Yet there were indications in 1993 that the General Assembly might be undergoing a transformation toward a more open, egalitarian style of legislative politics. Such a process had occurred in many other American legislatures (Ehrenhalt 1991). In Rhode Island, the change appeared to be traceable to the aftermath of a major crisis with overtones of political scandal: the collapse of the state's credit union insurance system in late 1989. While the system had been in private hands, it was state supervised. The collapse left many customers without access to their savings for months, had ripple effects throughout the state economy, and prompted a huge outcry against political leaders. State politicians were said to precipitate the crisis through poor oversight and too cozy relationships with credit union officials (Dodson 1993; Gurwitt 1994). The crisis apparently prompted an unusually large number of voluntary retirements from the General Assembly in 1992 (MacKay and Miller 1992). Such uncommonly high turnover in turn made possible the election of new "reform" leaders in both houses publicly committed to "opening up" the legislative process.

In recent years the Rhode Island General Assembly had been a virtual one-party legislature. Nearly 83 percent of lawmakers were Democrats in 1993, including thirty-nine of fifty state senators and eighty-five of one hundred members of the House of Representatives. As would be expected under such circumstances, the Democratic legislators were a very heterogeneous group, including many self-identified conservatives as well as more liberal lawmakers.[3]

With respect to automobile insurance reform, lawmakers in 1993 inherited an issue that had received considerable attention (if little definitive action) in previous years. Prior to that year, various no-fault bills had been introduced, but sponsors found it difficult to obtain hearings on the legislation and none came close to passage. In 1991 the legislature passed a bill requiring that drivers purchase automobile insurance; Rhode Island had been one of the few remaining North American jurisdictions without such a law. The compulsory insurance legislation created considerable controversy, with some arguing that insurance was unaffordable in the state. The General Assembly subsequently passed a bill to delay implementation, while requiring establishment of the Automobile Insurance Task Force to consider ways of lowering insurance rates. The Task Force was chaired by Sheldon Whitehouse, director of the Department of Business Regulation (DBR), and included representation from many interests including, among others, insurance companies, insurance agents, trial lawyers, medical providers, and consumer groups. The Task Force met regularly during the summer and fall of 1992. These meetings set the stage for the battle that followed.

THE BATTLE OVER INSURANCE REFORM
Players and Positions

In early 1993 Whitehouse announced DBR's support for a package of automobile insurance reform measures. The legislation was aimed at "reducing the cost of automobile insurance for Rhode Island's citizens," a goal said to be of great importance because insurance rates in Rhode Island were among the "highest in the nation" (Whitehouse 1993). The DBR package included a wide array of proposals in such diverse areas as insurance fraud prevention, contributory negligence, enforcement of the state's seat-belt requirement, and standards for drunk-driving convictions. Many of these proposals had received substantial support within the task force. The centerpiece of the DBR package, however, was effectively set aside in task force deliberations because it was too controversial: a proposal to institute a verbal threshold no-fault system modeled on that existing in New York. Adoption of a no-fault system accounted for the bulk of the projected savings from enacting the DBR package (Whitehouse 1993). A DBR-commissioned actuarial study of the impact of the proposed legislative package indicated that adoption of all measures whose financial impact could be estimated would result in an estimated 22 percent premium savings, with enactment of no-fault responsible for 15.3 percent of the savings (Tillinghast 1993).

Because of DBR's sponsorship, Whitehouse assumed the mantle of leader of the forces advocating no-fault. But he was not alone. The proposal quickly received support from the two insurance agents' asso-

The Battle Over Insurance Reform 77

ciations, which had long been favorable toward no-fault. The bill also received some immediate support from legislators, including Paul Kelly, the new leader of the State Senate. Kelly, who had carried unsuccessful no-fault legislation in the past, agreed to carry the enabling legislation for the DBR plan. A more junior legislator agreed to carry the House version of the legislation.

Interestingly, the insurance companies themselves were latecomers to support of the DBR's no-fault plan. Eventually the companies backed the proposal, contributing financial resources to the campaign to convince lawmakers. Some companies were also instrumental in a grassroots effort to stimulate constituency support of no-fault, which will be discussed further.

The no-fault plan was opposed by a loose coalition. At the center of the coalition were two groups: the Rhode Island Trial Lawyers Association and Ocean State Action, a consumer group with ties to organized labor. A source close to the trial lawyers indicated to me that defeat of no-fault was "the highest, absolutely highest" priority for that group. The same source acknowledged that the trial lawyers contributed up to $200,000 to fight no-fault, and some on the other side placed the figure higher. It was argued, however, that such spending was needed to counter the wealthy insurance companies, who could spend still more on behalf of no-fault legislation. At the same time some trial lawyers acknowledged that their opposition to no-fault was suspect, given attorneys' financial stake in preserving access to tort remedies. This may have explained why Ocean State Action was the more visible partner in the coalition opposed to no-fault.

The opposition did not simply stake out a position against no-fault. Led by Ocean State Action, the opposition offered what was claimed to be an alternative means of significantly lowering insurance rates. Modeled after California's Proposition 103, the ballot initiative passed in 1988, the plan called for "reform" of the insurance industry. The centerpiece of the plan was a requirement that insurance companies roll back insurance rates.

Governor Bruce Sundlun, a Democrat, did not take a visible position in the debate. While he was said to be supportive of no-fault, and while Whitehouse's leadership made the no-fault legislation "an Administration bill" (since Whitehouse was a governor's appointee), Sundlun himself remained at a distance from the fray.

Arguments and Tactics

Among those involved in the battle, there seems to have been a general consensus that legislators as a group were initially quite divided on the issue of no-fault. A source close to the trial lawyers acknowledged that attorney-legislators, who accounted for over 25 percent of membership in the General Assembly, formed a base of opposition. The task for opponents was to solidify and broaden this base. There was not an equivalent base of support for no-fault since only a handful of lawmakers had any association with the insurance industry, and some of these legislators were precluded from voting on the issue based on a ruling of the Rhode Island Ethics Commission.[4]

Both sides engaged in extensive efforts to "educate" legislators about the merits of their positions. These attempts occurred during lengthy public hearings held by the corporation committees of the respective houses. Educational efforts also occurred during private meetings between lawmakers and partisans in the insurance reform controversy. At such meetings lawmakers were commonly provided with written materials containing data and other information that was purported to support claims made by debate partisans. Much time was also spent attempting to counter the "misinformation" from the other side.

Additionally, both sides brought in "experts" to buttress their arguments, several of whom were from outside the state. These experts testified at committee hearings, and some also met with individual lawmakers. The side favoring no-fault drew upon the deputy superintendent of insurance for New York, as well as the actuary who conducted the cost study of the DBR plan. Ocean State Action, the most visible group on the opposition side, brought in Ralph Nader, as well as a Nader ally who had been the chief sponsor of California's Proposition 103.

As a result of the educational efforts, virtually none of the lawmakers I interviewed indicated that information was lacking. It was more common for legislators to complain of being deluged with information without adequate time to digest it and/or to express worry about the biases in the information. One lawmaker characterized the situation as "information overload." Several lawmakers expressed concern that all the information they obtained came from lobbyists and interest groups, rather than from "neutral sources."

Significantly, much of the debate pertained to competing claims about the potential effectiveness of no-fault and of legislation modeled on Proposition 103; the two sides offered sharply different views of what would happen under the competing proposals. The opposing sides buttressed their larger points with subtly different supporting arguments. Thus, for example, advocates focused on the experience in New York, contending that appropriate lessons could only be drawn on systems most similar to the one proposed for Rhode Island. Opponents, however, focused on the experience in no-fault states more generally.

The Battle Over Insurance Reform

It was also common for partisans to attack the credibility of groups on the other side. Undoubtedly because of their perceived unpopularity, insurance companies and trial lawyers were the main targets. No-fault opponents were especially likely to bash the insurance companies, while some proponents attacked the trial lawyers. This was evident in Nader's 1 April testimony before the House Corporations Committee. After slamming insurance companies for waste, inefficiency, and hostility toward customers, and arguing that implementation of no-fault was merely a means of enhancing industry profits, he stated:[5]

> [. . .] If you're getting the impression I'm very critical of the insurance companies, I want to tell you that I'm not entirely critical. I happen to think they're among our most religious corporations. I say that because they believe so many events in life are acts of God.

Similarly, during a 18 February hearing before the Senate Corporations Committee, an insurance company representative testified as follows:[6]

> Let's face it. Any time you put forward a plan to reduce costs, somebody's ox is going to be gored. In this case it's the trial lawyers' ox. And they [sic] are very powerful[. . . .] In lobbying on this issue [in Connecticut], I've been told by [attorney] legislators, behind closed doors, that if this type of legislation, no-fault legislation, were to go through, they wouldn't be able to send their kids to college. Now, it's not whether this type of legislation is a good thing for the people of Connecticut, or in this case the people of Rhode Island, it's how it affects their pocketbook[s].

In addition to attempting to persuade legislators directly, debate partisans attempted to influence lawmakers indirectly through public relations campaigns and grass-roots efforts. For example, a group calling itself "Lawyers for Consumer Rights" took out a full page advertisement in the 28 March edition of the *Providence Sunday Journal*, with large headlines proclaiming "Consumers Are Finding Fault with No-Fault." The advertisement accused the insurance industry of pushing no-fault to make even more money, claimed that eight of ten states with the highest insurance rates had no-fault systems, and argued that under no-fault "the guilty and innocent are treated alike." Meantime one insurance company, headquartered in Rhode Island, sent a letter to its customers indicating that implementation of no-fault would lead to lower premiums and urging customers to contact their legislators. Some lawmakers indicated that this effort had indeed resulted in many letters and phone calls.

Legislative Action

The Kelly no-fault bill made progress in the Senate. By a vote of twelve to three, it was approved by the Corporations Committee on 1 April. Sensing insufficient support from the full Senate, however, Kelly decided to substitute provisions for a choice no-fault system for the mandatory no-fault provisions in the original bill. The bill was considered in the full Senate on 11 May. Kelly's proposed changes were approved, and he and his allies narrowly beat back an attempt to recommit the bill to committee.

Debate in the full Senate was heated and dominated by no-fault opponents. Senators against no-fault questioned the savings from the legislation, attacked the insurance companies, and argued that cost reductions could better be achieved by reforming the industry. Following is a sample of some of the comments:

> You've got to look at [the fact that] the insurance industry has escalating premiums built into the structure [of the insurance system....Everyone who testified during public hearings], whether for or against no-fault, said that the insurance industry has to reform. And everyone in the legislature has a responsibility to ensure that [such] reform takes place. I don't see one iota in [the amendments or bill] that reforms the industry. Nothing is taking place. [Insurance companies] are still operating on a cost-plus basis[....] Unless the insurance industry is forced to reform itself [you're] not going to get the savings projected[....] This [legislation] is simply a way to save face for an industry that will not reform itself[....] If you vote for this[....] bill, you are simply voting for the insurance industry.[7]
>
> The bill talks of rate reductions[....] which is a fallacy. You're going to try to convince me that you're going to try to bind an insurance company's rates? It hasn't been done in the history of this country. You're dealing with the largest[....] lobbying force[....] I don't care who the director of business regulation is[....] There's no way in heaven that man is going to tell an insurance carrier that he can't [set rates] the way he wants to [set rates...] without an antitrust bill that puts real teeth to the matter [....] So who's winning in this whole scenario of insurance reform? Is it insurance reform? Or is it: how [can] we make more profits [for] an industry that has become so powerful that it can manipulate and control even the Congress of the United States?[...] What are we talking about ladies and gentlemen? Are we protecting the rights of the individual? Or are we protecting—or increasing—the profits of a large industrial conglomerate?[8]
>
> So that the public doesn't think this [no-fault bill] is the only possible reform for the high premiums we face, there has been another proposal based on reforms in California that would address the true causes of high insurance rates. It provides for real regulatory reform. It provides for real competition in the insurance market[....] It's a wide-ranging and comprehensive proposal.[9]

Explaining Legislative Decisions

After considerable discussion, one of the most telling events in the no-fault saga occurred. Senator Bradford Gorham offered what he called a "truth in insurance" amendment to the Kelly bill. Arguing that it was necessary to hold proponents to their promises of premium savings, Gorham proposed requiring that insurance companies reduce rates by 20 percent the first year, and allowing percentage premium increases in the subsequent five years only up to the rate of change in the Consumer Price Index.[10] The chairman of the Senate Corporations Committee, a staunch no-fault supporter, bitterly denounced this proposal as a "killer amendment." He claimed that this proposal could lead to company insolvency, since increases in actual insurance costs could exceed the general rate of inflation. Nevertheless, the amendment passed thirty-one to fifteen. The amended bill was subsequently approved thirty to seventeen. The Corporations Committee chairman, saying he "would not be part of a ruse," voted against the amended version of the bill.

Reaction to the events on the Senate floor was swift. The *Providence Journal-Bulletin* (1993) editorialized against the action on the Senate floor, accusing Gorham of using a "subtle technique" to "smother no-fault insurance without appearing to do so." Gorham (1993) denied the charge in a rebuttal article, claiming he was engaged in a "straight forward" effort to "ensure that consumers in Rhode Island would receive the promised rate reduction." Meantime several insurance companies, worried about the implications of the amended bill, withdrew their support for the plan.[11]

In the House of Representatives, no-fault legislation languished in the Corporations Committee. Then in the closing days of the 1993 session, the committee failed to pass two versions of no-fault legislation. At the same time, the Ocean State Action-backed bill received the committee's approval. (That bill contained portions of the industry reform plan modeled after California's Proposition 103.) However, that legislation was not pushed further in the Senate and remained on the House floor after the General Assembly adjourned.

EXPLAINING LEGISLATIVE DECISIONS: RHODE ISLAND VERSUS PENNSYLVANIA

The key puzzle that must now be addressed is why similar reform efforts succeeded in Pennsylvania and failed in Rhode Island. My focus will remain on that question during the remainder of this chapter. I also will give some consideration to how both Rhode Island and Pennsylvania compared to other American states.

Suppose pressure theory was sufficient to explain why, at roughly the same time, Pennsylvania adopted a form of no-fault while Rhode

Island and other states did not. Given the facts presented thus far (including information indicating that the insurance companies opposed the Casey plan in 1989–90, while they typically supported no-fault in Pennsylvania, Rhode Island, and elsewhere), an argument of that type would need to make some or all of the following claims:

- Pennsylvania consumers' actual or potential (à la Arnold) concern about insurance rates was relatively high.
- Compared to Rhode Island and other states, the influence of trial lawyers in Pennsylvania was relatively small, and/or trial attorneys were not as intensely concerned about events in Pennsylvania.
- The governor's active involvement in the Pennsylvania battle effectively increased pressure on lawmakers and made support for the Casey plan inevitable.

The first claim can be dismissed most quickly. Pennsylvania consumers did face high and rising rates and were consequently quite angry—but this was also true in states where reform plans failed, including Rhode Island. If anything, objective indicators imply there should have been even *more* pressure for Rhode Island lawmakers (and legislators in a few other states) than for Pennsylvania lawmakers to do something decisive about the rates problem. Rhode Island ranked fourth in average insurance expenditures in 1990, while Pennsylvania ranked tenth.[12] Insurance rates also had been climbing faster in Rhode Island than in Pennsylvania in the late 1980s (NAIC 1993).

The second claim warrants greater consideration, although ultimately it too appears insufficient to explain the cross-state differences. There is little reason to believe that in Pennsylvania trial lawyers were either not intensely interested in auto insurance or not especially influential. The PTLA was as involved in insurance battles as trial lawyer organizations in other states. Objective measures suggest the "stakes" for trial lawyers were high in *both* Pennsylvania and Rhode Island. Notably, one study (All-Industry Research Advisory Council 1988) showed that the former state ranked ninth in the portion of automobile accident victims represented by an attorney (49.2 percent), while the latter ranked eighth (49.3 percent). The little comparative cross-state work on interest-group influence also indicates that trial lawyers were a relatively effective force in Pennsylvania (Crotty 1993; Thomas 1993).

Yet perhaps it is a mistake to examine only the behavior of trial lawyers *outside* the legislature. Given their traditional numbers and influence, an argument can be made that attorney influence is most effectively channeled through lawyer-legislators (see Miller 1995). In-

Explaining Legislative Decisions 83

deed, some past empirical research indicates that lawyer-lawmakers vote differently with respect to the specific issue of no-fault insurance (Dyer 1976).

But if this argument was to explain the different outcome in Pennsylvania, it would help if that state had ranked low in terms of the portion of attorneys in the state legislature. That was not the case. Shortly before the period covered by my study, a national survey showed that 16 percent of all American state legislators were attorneys (Squire 1992). Yet 21 percent of all Pennsylvania lawmakers were attorneys in 1989 (while 25 percent of Rhode Island legislators were attorneys in 1993).[13]

Nevertheless, at least if the comparison is limited to Rhode Island and Pennsylvania, it might be contended that lawyer-legislators in the former state gave more consideration to their interests as attorneys. The argument would be that in a nonprofessional institution, lawmakers primarily define themselves in terms of their occupations outside the legislature. Lawyer-legislators are therefore more apt to represent the interests of their occupational group.

There is some evidence to support this argument. As shown in table 5.1, Rhode Island lawyer-legislators provided a solid bulwark of opposition to no-fault. In four key 1993 votes, not a single lawyer-legislator cast a single vote in favor of strong no-fault legislation. By contrast, Pennsylvania's lawyer-lawmakers were more divided on the question. As shown in table 5.2, over one-third of lawyer-legislators in the Pennsylvania House of Representatives voted against the first conference committee report in 1989 (the alternative package without tort reform provisions, condemned by Governor Casey and his allies, and defeated by the House membership in a surprise vote). Lawyer-legislators also were as likely as other lawmakers to support the second conference committee package, which reflected the agreements hammered out by the Casey administration and other interested parties. And as noted previously, two Pennsylvania lawyer-legislators (Representatives Richard Hayden and Stephen Freind) played a leadership role on behalf of the legislation that would become Act 6.[14]

Yet while solid opposition from lawyer-legislators may help to explain the different results in Rhode Island, it is difficult to see that as a sufficient explanation. As shown in table 5.1, a majority of Rhode Island senators who were not lawyers voted in favor of the Gorham amendment. A majority of nonlawyer representatives voted against no-fault in the House Corporations Committee.

Moreover, if anything, nonattorney legislators in Rhode Island should have been *less* concerned about support from trial lawyers than nonattorney lawmakers in Pennsylvania. Simply put, trial-lawyer

TABLE 5.1.
Support for Strong No-Fault Legislation among Lawyer-Legislators and Other Lawmakers in Rhode Island

RESULTS OF KEY 1993 VOTES*

Vote within Senate Corporations Committee		Senate Floor Vote on Motion to Recommit No-Fault Bill	
Lawyers	Others	Lawyers	Others
(N=1)	(N=14)	(N=12)	(N=31)
0%	86	0	74

Senate Floor Vote on Major Weakening Amendment (the "Gorham Amendment")		Vote within House Corporations Committee	
Lawyers	Others	Lawyers	Others
(N=12)	(N=32)	(N=2)	(N=12)
0	47	0	42

*Votes on the following motions were used to construct this table: (a) motion in the Senate Corporations Committee on 1 April 1993 to recommend approval of Senator Paul Kelly's no-fault legislation, SB 529; (b) motion in the full Senate on 11 May 1993 to recommend that SB 529 be recommitted to the Senate Corporations Committee; (c) motion by Senator Bradford Gorham to amend SB 529 (substance of the amendment described in the main text); and (d) motion before the House Corporations Committee on 15 July 1993 to recommend approval of Representative Brian Kennedy's no-fault bill, H 5634. Abstentions were excluded.

backing would seem more important for political careers in Pennsylvania. Legislative districts in that state were much larger than those in Rhode Island.[15] Districts in the latter state also tended to be physically compact, given the state's tiny geographical size. For these reasons a Rhode Island lawmaker seeking reelection needed relatively little of the campaign funds and other types of campaign support that could be offered by a well-endowed group. Furthermore, legislative seats themselves were not as valuable in Rhode Island, measured in terms of monetary benefits, perquisites, and opportunities for political advancement.[16]

The claim about gubernatorial influence needs the most careful consideration. There can be no doubt that as a state chief executive, Governor Casey was unusually involved in the automobile insurance reform battle (although a few other governors were highly active on

Explaining Legislative Decisions

TABLE 5.2.
Support for Strong No-Fault Legislation among Lawyer-Legislators and Other Lawmakers in Pennsylvania

RESULTS OF KEY 1989–1990 VOTES*

House Floor Vote on First Conference Committee Report		House Floor Vote on Second Conference Committee Report	
Lawyers	Others	Lawyers	Others
(N=38)	(N=162)	(N=37)	(N=160)
37%	65	78	79

Senate Floor Vote on Second Conference Committee Report	
Lawyers	Others
(N=15)	(N=35)
93	89

*Votes on the following measures were used to construct this table: (a) House floor vote on approval of the first conference committee report on HB 121, 12 December 1989 (the alternative insurance reform measure opposed by the Casey administration; a "no" vote was interpreted as supporting strong no-fault); (b) House floor vote on approval of the second conference committee report on HB 121, 7 February 1990 (containing the Casey proposal); a "yes" vote was interpreted as supporting strong no-fault; and (c) Senate vote on approval of the second conference committee report on HB 121, 7 February 1990. Abstentions were excluded.

It should be noted that the House vote on the first conference committee report was the most telling. The second conference committee report ratified the agreements reached between the administration and various interested parties.

this issue; see especially the discussion of Hawaii in chapter 7). The contrast with Rhode Island is particularly stark, since Governor Sundlun remained on the sidelines in that state.

However, a few problems with the "gubernatorial pressure" theory must be emphasized. The first is conceptual. In separation-of-powers systems (especially under the primary election model that has come to dominate elections in the United States), governors generally cannot directly influence the political careers of legislators. Governors usually cannot prevent lawmakers they dislike from being renominated, or from winning nomination to higher office. If governors are to affect legislators' careers, it will generally be through the indirect route of inspiring greater pressure on lawmakers from constituency groups. But it may be difficult to distinguish such influence from the power of the governor's ideas, since it is likely that the governor will be "making a case" to lawmakers themselves at the same time. That is, a governor may influence a lawmaker (a) by "turning up the constituency heat" or (b) by convincing the legislator that the governor's position holds merit. Only the former path falls under the pressure theory rubric.

Even if we interpret Casey's influence in Pennsylvania solely in terms of activating constituents to pressure lawmakers (and it is not clear we would want to do so), difficulties arise in seeing this as a factor sufficient to explain the different policy choice in that state. Returning to points stressed in chapter 4, Casey lost some key battles prior to the end of 1989. Alternative plans existed for lawmakers who wanted to mollify angry constituents, some of whom did not require consumers to make any painful choices. Yet ultimately lawmakers embraced the administration's plan.

In short, pressure theory appears insufficient to explain the different paths taken by lawmakers in Pennsylvania and those taken in Rhode Island and elsewhere. I contend that we need also to draw on the politics of ideas. It is reasonable to believe that, at least by the end of 1989, Pennsylvania legislators were more likely to think that the executive branch's plan was the "strong medicine that was needed" than were Rhode Island lawmakers. It is also reasonable to suppose that Pennsylvania legislators more thoroughly embraced the Pogo Story (and rejected the Profiteering Story) than did lawmakers in Rhode Island and perhaps those in other states as well. The rationale and evidence on behalf of this argument are as follows:

- If lawmakers used the position of the "bad guys" (i.e., special interests) as a cue to what was good for consumers generally, their task was more complicated in Rhode Island than in Pennsylvania. (For an argument that ordinary citizens use cues of that kind, see Lupia 1994.) In Pennsylvania all the major interests were opposed to the Casey plan, while in Rhode Island they were divided. Moreover, Ocean State Action, a "public interest" group, opposed the DBR proposal in Rhode Island. There was no equivalent group in Pennsylvania opposing the Casey administration's plan.
- In both states the respective administrations offered a Pogo Story explanation for the "insurance problem." In Rhode Island, however, Ocean State Action explicitly offered a competing diagnosis that was completely consistent with all the premises of the Profiteering Story. Blame was placed squarely on the insurance companies, and the solution was said to be "industry reform." Ocean

State Action and its allies (notably Nader) clearly rejected the notion that consumers needed to "trade off" any benefits to receive cuts in insurance premiums.
- While the respective administrations estimated substantial consumer savings for both the DBR plan and the Casey proposal, the savings were more explicitly referenced in the Pennsylvania implementing legislation. This may have helped to assure lawmakers that savings would materialize (as noted earlier, the Gorham amendment in Rhode Island attacked exactly this issue).
- Unlike their Rhode Island counterparts, Pennsylvania lawmakers operated in the shadow of what was widely seen as failed legislative efforts to address the rates problem. That is, members of the Pennsylvania Assembly often discussed widely touted proposals passed in earlier years that actually made matters worse. By contrast, even floor debate on reform proposals was rather new in Rhode Island, where no-fault plans had tended to die in committee, often without hearings.
- During floor debate, Rhode Island lawmakers themselves were much more likely to articulate arguments consistent with the Profiteering Story than were Pennsylvania legislators. I have already quoted extensively from the floor debate in Rhode Island, and these quotes suggest that many lawmakers were comfortable attributing the rates problem to insurance company profiteering. It is likely that some Rhode Island lawmakers took comments from their lawyer-legislator colleagues with a grain of salt, given the well-understood opposition of trial lawyers to no-fault. Yet it is interesting to note that remarks consistent with the Profiteering Story (whether by lawyer-legislators or others) largely went unchallenged in Rhode Island.[17]

CONCLUSION

Arguing that the politics of ideas shaped the policy decisions in Rhode Island and Pennsylvania is not the same thing as arguing that lawmakers chose wisely—a point that is sometimes obscured in the literature on policy deliberation (see Lascher 1996). Indeed, to the extent that decisions in Rhode Island were influenced by many legislators' embrace of the Profiteering Story and rejection of the Pogo Story, there is cause for concern. Ocean State Action and its allies may have been convincing. But their arguments rested on flimsy premises.

NOTES TO CHAPTER 5

1. The Rhode Island bill was a more traditional choice plan, in that mandatory first party benefits were to be higher for those selecting the no-fault option. As noted in chapter 4, in Pennsylvania mandatory first party coverage was identical for people selecting either the full-tort or limited-tort options; what differed were premium levels and entitlement to sue for pain and suffering.

2. This characterization of the General Assembly is based mainly on my extensive discussions with a large number of people familiar with Rhode Island politics. It is consistent with journalistic descriptions; see Dodson 1993; Gurwitt 1994; Riggs 1993.

3. Survey of Rhode Island lawmakers I conducted in the summer of 1993.

4. The ruling was contained in Commission Advisory No. 13, 26 March 1992.

5. These statements were transcribed from a videotape of the hearing. I am grateful to the Capitol Television office of the Rhode Island General Assembly for providing me with the videotape.

6. This testimony was from Clifford Licht, representing Nationwide Insurance Company.

7. These comments were from Senator John Orabona.

8. These comments were from Senator John Bevilacqua.

9. These comments were from Senator Myrth York.

10. In a conversation with me, a no-fault opponent acknowledged that the Gorham amendment had been planned in advance of the floor debate, and that an advocate for the trial lawyers was involved in the plan. Gorham was himself an attorney.

It should also be noted that there was some ambiguity about whether the Gorham amendment applied only to people who chose the no-fault option, or to all consumers. To the extent the latter was the case, the amendment was especially likely to lead to instances in which insurance companies were required to pass along savings without comparable reductions in operating costs.

11. The insurance companies may also have been intimidated by threats from the leadership in the House of Representatives. According to a number of sources, in a closed-door meeting, House leaders opposed to no-fault threatened to use their influence to secure passage of legislation unfavorable to the insurance industry, unless the insurance companies backed away from their support for no-fault. In any event, the companies' withdrawal of support caused anger among some no-fault supporters, who accused them of cowardice.

12. True, as noted earlier, Philadelphia's insurance rates were perhaps the highest in the nation. But it is not clear that this was as beneficial for the reform effort as would have been the case if high rates had been more uniformly distributed across Pennsylvania. Indeed, the sentiment was sometimes expressed that there was only a "Philadelphia problem," not a statewide problem.

13. The Pennsylvania figure was calculated from Doukas 1989. The Rhode Island figure was calculated from Impact Communications 1993.

Notes to Chapter 5

14. Another question that might arise is whether there was a difference between the two states with respect to the leadership positions held by lawyer-legislators. In fact, the two states were similar in this respect; lawyer-lawmakers held key leadership positions in both Rhode Island and Pennsylvania. If anything, attorneys were less dominant in the Rhode Island leadership. In that state the two top Democratic positions in the House were held by lawyers, while the two top positions in the Senate were held by nonlawyers (recall that the Democrats had lopsided majorities in both houses). In Pennsylvania, where the political parties were closely divided, the president pro tempore and majority leader in the Senate were attorneys, as were the Speaker, majority floor leader, and minority floor leader in the House.

15. Members of the Pennsylvania House represented about 59,000 people, while state senators represented about 240,000 constituents. By contrast, state representatives in the Rhode Island House represented about 10,000 people, while state senators represented about 20,000 constituents.

16. The Rhode Island General Assembly is a classic example of what Peverill Squire (1988) has termed a "dead-end" legislature, offering neither high levels of compensation nor a relatively large number of opportunities to use the legislative position as a springboard.

17. Senate Corporations Committee chairman William Irons implicitly made a Pogo Story–type argument in opposing the Gorham amendment. Aside from his remarks, none of the other arguments made by no-fault supporters could easily be interpreted as offering a defense of the Pogo Story or an attack on the Profiteering Story.

6
Different Reform Regimes: Ontario

> Our main concern was finding a product that worked.
> —A participant in the decision-making process
> that led to Ontario's no-fault automobile
> insurance system[1]

Previous chapters make clear that the path to automobile insurance reform generally, and no-fault insurance specifically, has been a difficult one in the United States. The discussion of the "Pennsylvania exception" only further underscores this point. Enactment of Act 6 required a strong dose of executive leadership and circumstances making it easy for legislators to conclude that the Casey reform package would work. Even then (and for better or worse), Pennsylvania made only a partial movement toward no-fault, enacting a "choice" law rather than establishing a mandatory no-fault system.

For those familiar only with the U.S. experience, a look across the country's northern border can therefore be startling. During the period I studied, while American automobile insurance laws were characterized by stasis, laws in some Canadian provinces were characterized by dramatic change. Ontario's experience is especially striking, featuring what to American eyes may seem a rather dizzying series of policy shifts. From the middle of the 1980s to the middle of the 1990s, the provincial legislature enacted a number of far-reaching proposals, including but not limited to enactment of a no-fault scheme that went well beyond anything that had been tried in the United States. More specifically, various Ontario governments

- moved to stringent price regulation from a status quo in which insurance companies were free to set their own rates;
- enacted a law requiring a uniform rate classification system, and banning age, sex, and marital status as considerations in setting rates;
- subsequently passed a law overturning the uniform classification scheme before it had a chance to take effect;

Different Reform Regimes: Ontario

- adopted a verbal threshold no-fault system with the wording of the restriction on litigation "much stronger and tighter than any existing verbal threshold in the United States" (O'Donnell 1991, 202); and
- subsequently enacted a law placing further restrictions on the right to sue, while substantially increasing no-fault benefits for automobile accident victims.

Along the way, serious consideration was given to moving to a public automobile insurance system. And by 1996 the new Progressive Conservative Party government was planning another major change in the automobile insurance system, affecting both benefit levels and access to the tort system (*Thompson's World Insurance News* 1996).

The major alterations in policy direction provide an illuminating contrast with events in my other case study jurisdictions. Ontario automobile insurance also is of intrinsic importance. To use a football metaphor, this is "the big game" with respect to Canadian public policy in the insurance arena. Automobile insurance is "by far the biggest segment of the insurance industry" in Canada, and Ontario, as the country's most populous and most wealthy province, has the largest insurance market (Sutton 1991, 27). It was estimated that in 1989 Ontario auto insurance represented a full one-quarter of the premiums collected by general insurers in Canada in 1989 (Baetz 1993). The importance of the Ontario automobile insurance issue is reflected in political commentary. To illustrate, each of two book-length studies of how the New Democratic Party (NDP) governed the province devoted a full chapter to the battle over public automobile insurance (Monahan 1995, ch. 3; Walkom 1994, ch. 5).

In this chapter I describe and attempt to explain the policy changes in Ontario, focusing especially on the Liberal Party's move from a rate control strategy to a no-fault insurance strategy. I contend that the policy shifts can, in part, be linked to acceptance of different causal stories. That is, Ontario's political leaders moved toward fully embracing a version of the Pogo Story, which attributed the "rates crisis" to spiraling claims costs rather than the willful acts of the unpopular insurance industry. Acceptance of the Pogo Story prompted political leaders to focus on options that would decisively lower claims costs. A strong no-fault system fit the bill.

Another factor made decision making in Ontario very different from decision making in Pennsylvania and Rhode Island: the existence of the Westminster parliamentary system. I contend that this system served as a powerful mechanism for Ontario elected officials concerned about the broad middle class. However, I will refrain from discussing this theme further until chapter 7, in which I compare as groups the Canadian provinces and American states. My focus in the present chapter will remain on Ontario, and the province-specific factors that might explain the policy decisions that were made there.

Undoubtedly because of its intrinsic importance, the battle in Ontario is the most well chronicled of the quarrels over automobile insurance reform that have occurred in North American jurisdictions. There are a number of good case studies covering different periods in the controversy (Atkinson and Nigol 1989; Baetz 1993; Devlin 1993; Feldthusen 1990; Monahan 1995, ch. 3; O'Donnell 1991; Walkom 1994, ch. 5). There are also official government reports that provide extensive background information (see especially Osborne 1988). Consequently, this chapter will draw relatively more upon secondary sources than have previous ones. The secondary sources are supplemented by a number of primary sources described in the appendix.

CONTEXT FOR THE 1989–1990 NO-FAULT BILL

The Ontario Political System

As in other Canadian provinces, executive power in Ontario rests with the head of the provincial legislature (the premier) and a cabinet of ministers with responsibility for overseeing government agencies. The legislature is unicameral, and as of the late 1980s it included 130 members. Each lawmaker represents a single member district (or "riding," as the term is used in Canada). In recent times all legislators have hailed from a political party, and party discipline has been strong. Indeed, Graham White (1989, 77–78) has written,

> Party cohesion in the Ontario legislature is, as Samuel Beer remarked in describing the British House of Commons in the 1960s, "so close to 100 per cent that there was no longer any point in measuring it." A study of voting records of the Thirty-second Parliament (1981–84) showed that, except for a handful of items of private members' business, all recorded votes were party votes, defined as votes wherein at least 90 per cent of each party's [members] voted together. The results would not have been much different had the criterion been 100 per cent, for many sessions pass without a single member's voting against his party in the House on a matter of any import.

Ontario has been politically competitive of late, with three major political parties commanding significant support. The left leaning NDP, centrist Liberal Party, and moderate to right leaning Progressive Conservative Party each have governed the province within the past ten

Context for the 1989–1990 No-Fault Bill 93

years.[2] The Liberals formed a minority government after the 1985 election, upon reaching an accord with the NDP committing the government to supporting various NDP-backed initiatives (White 1989, 10–13). In 1987 the Liberals won an overwhelming election victory, obviating the need for a coalition with the NDP. At the time in which the Liberals' no-fault bill was proposed, the party held 94 of 130 legislative seats, while the NDP held nineteen seats and the Progressive Conservatives held seventeen seats. Then in the fall of 1990 the NDP won an upset electoral victory, taking control of the provincial government for the first time in the party's history. The NDP government lasted until 1995 when the Progressive Conservatives assumed power after winning an outright majority of legislative seats.

Automobile Insurance as a Major Political Issue

By the latter part of the 1980s automobile insurance had become one of Ontario's most contentious political issues. The middle part of the decade had seen rapidly increasing premiums (Osborne 1988). The rate hikes triggered widespread public anger, claims that insurance had become unaffordable for particular groups such as young drivers, and demands for government action. The political parties attempted to position themselves advantageously on the issue (Atkinson and Nigol 1989; Baetz 1993; Feldthusen 1990). According to some commentators, automobile insurance was in fact "the main election issue" in 1987 (see for example Baetz 1993).

In the midst of the 1987 campaign, an event occurred that would have long-term significance. The Ontario premier, David Peterson, indicated that he had a specific plan for reducing insurance premiums; he did not provide details.[3] In actuality the Liberal government had been studying various proposals but had not settled on an alternative. After the Liberals' huge election win, which likely was buoyed by Peterson's claim, government officials believed they had an obligation to make good on the premier's promise of effecting rate reductions. As one person involved in discussion of policy alternatives put it to me, Peterson had "boxed them in," effectively eliminating consideration of any options that would allow the types of rate increases that had been seen earlier in the decade.

Even before the 1987 election the Liberals made initial, admittedly stop-gap efforts to attack the rates problem, all of which moved the government in the direction of tighter regulatory control over the private-sector insurance industry. More specifically, in April of 1987 the minister of financial institutions, attacking the track record of the insurance industry and accusing it of engaging in discriminatory practices, announced the government's support for a freeze on insurance premiums. The minister also announced the government's backing of legislation to enforce the freeze, provide for the creation of an auto insurance board to control rates, and roll back rates for young drivers. Following the industry's voluntary, if grudging, compliance with the proposed rate freeze, the government refrained from pushing the legislation further; it died at the adjournment of the 1987 session.

Subsequent to the election, the Liberals came back with legislation that appeared to signal continued commitment to stringent regulation of industry practices and price controls as a means of addressing the public's rate concerns. The government introduced the Ontario Automobile Insurance Board (OAIB) Act, establishing the OAIB as a rate-control agency. The OAIB was to be given extensive powers and was also to be charged with using a uniform classification system (i.e., a system for equalizing rates across categories of drivers). The act was approved in February of 1988, and the agency began operation shortly thereafter.

Behind the scenes, however, a small executive committee consisting of the premier and senior ministers began meeting regularly to consider various other means of addressing the rates problem on a long-term basis. Murray Elston, the new minister for financial institutions, had lead responsibility for presenting and evaluating the options. Staff from the ministry gathered information about automobile insurance regimes in other jurisdictions, such as Quebec's pure no-fault system and the verbal threshold no-fault system used in Michigan and New York. Actuaries were hired to develop cost estimates of possible ways of reducing rates. The executive committee as a whole debated the proposals.

Meantime the initial Liberal Party initiatives seem to have diffused some of the public's anger. Then in December of 1988 the release of a government-commissioned consultant's report, known as the "Mercer Report" for the name of the consulting firm, appears to have stirred the public's anger about insurance rates once again. The Mercer Report indicated that the combination of a rate freeze and spiraling increases in claims expenses had left automobile insurance premiums—widely considered "too high"—priced well below costs. The Mercer Report recommended that insurance premiums be allowed to increase by 35 to 40 percent.[4] This controversial recommendation earned front page newspaper coverage (see for example Barnes 1988). The public responded to the prospect of further premium hikes by deluging the newly created OAIB with phone calls of protest. A leader of a citizens campaign against rate increases, emphasizing the "great distrust of the insurance industry," went so far as delivering to Premier Peterson a

Context for the 1989-1990 No-Fault Bill

suitcase of protest petitions with fifty thousand signatures. In response to the outcry, Peterson was forced to defend his government's actions before the provincial legislature (Gooderham 1988; *Globe and Mail* 1989).

The Mercer Report was followed by a few turbulent months of public debate, while in private the Liberal government moved toward a policy recommendation. Early in 1989 Minister Elston requested that the OAIB conduct hearings on no-fault and other alternatives. The hearings were held and produced voluminous testimony, culminating in a July report. The OAIB provided only a lukewarm endorsement of no-fault, contending that no-fault would have some equity benefits, but challenging the idea that such a system would lead to premium reductions. Yet by the spring Elston himself signaled to the press his belief that no-fault was necessary to control costs; he later expressed disagreement with the conclusions of the OAIB report (Story 1989; Walker 1989a).

During the same period the Liberal government backed away from some of its previous positions, while maintaining others (see especially O'Donnell 1991). In particular, the government (for reasons discussed further in a following section) abandoned the plan to equalize rates across categories of drivers through a uniform classification system. An announcement to that effect was made in the spring of 1989, in the midst of OAIB's preparations to implement the new system. Legislation implementing suspension of the uniform classification system, and effectively overturning much of the OAIB's work, was enacted in July of that year. Yet the government continued its public commitment to price ceilings. Simultaneous with the announcement of abandonment of the uniform classification system, Elston indicated that insurance companies would be limited to a 7.6 percent increase in premiums, a figure significantly below even that which had been recommended by the OAIB. Insurance company officials expressed shock and dismay at this decision (Brett 1989a).

Prior Attention to No-Fault and Other Alternatives

No-fault was scarcely a new idea in Ontario in 1989. Various studies addressing the topic had been commissioned, with mixed findings. In 1986 the Liberal government appointed economist David Slater to head a task force to consider solutions to problems created by soaring liability premiums in a number of areas, including but not limited to automobile insurance. The Slater Report recommended a pure no-fault system for automobile insurance, while indicating that a threshold no-fault system was preferable to the existing tort regime. The Liberals subsequently commissioned another study aimed more specifically at assessing the best system for compensating automobile accident victims. Justice Coulter Osborne from the Supreme Court of Ontario conducted the study. The Osborne Report, released in February 1988, recommended against both pure and threshold no-fault, although it supported expansion of first party accident benefits.

Other alternatives to the status quo had been widely discussed as well. In particular, the option of moving to a public automobile insurance system surfaced regularly. The NDP (and its predecessor, the Cooperative Commonwealth Federation) had long advocated such a system, and NDP governments had in fact established public automobile insurance in Manitoba and Saskatchewan. While the original rationale for public automobile insurance was based on the social democratic belief that all financial machinery ought to be controlled by the public, over time the justification had shifted to the idea that public systems were less expensive (Monahan 1995). For example, the NDP emphasized the cost argument during the 1987 Ontario election campaign.

Advocates of public automobile insurance claimed that there were economies of scale in the industry and that a public monopoly could deliver the same services as a private system, but with lower overhead costs. These claims were controversial. After examining systems in other provinces, Justice Osborne (1988) concluded that there was no "clear and convincing evidence of efficiency gains" under a public monopoly. He recommended against Ontario moving toward public automobile insurance.

THE BATTLE OVER NO-FAULT INSURANCE

Players and Positions

On 15 September 1989 Minister Elston announced the government's proposal to adopt a verbal threshold no-fault system, to be known as the Ontario Motorist Protection Plan (OMPP). Under the OMPP, lawsuits for "pain and suffering" were to be limited to instances in which accident victims were permanently or seriously injured, as defined in statute. To compensate for the restrictions on lawsuits, accident victims would be entitled to receive enhanced first party benefits, such as $450 per week in income replacement and up to $500,000 in reimbursement for medical care and rehabilitation expenses. According to Elston, the new system was necessary to forestall premium increases of 30 to 35 percent (MacLeod 1989). The government followed the announcement with introduction of implementing legislation.

The Liberals' plan had the strong backing of the insurance industry, including representatives of both insurance companies and insurance

The Battle over No-Fault Insurance

brokers (Brett 1989b). In fact, the Insurance Bureau of Canada (IBC), the major trade association for the nation's private insurance companies, earlier had proposed its own verbal threshold no-fault scheme. Dubbed "smart no-fault," the plan was pushed in newspaper and television advertisements in the spring of 1987 (Baetz 1993). While smart no-fault did not receive governmental support at the time it was advanced, the later OMPP proposal looked very similar, as one person closely involved in developing the industry plan emphasized in an interview. This is not to say that IBC staff actually drafted the government's plan, as some critics suggested. Rather, it appears that those drafting the OMPP found the verbal threshold system an attractive model.

The government's plan was strongly and vocally opposed by a coalition led by attorney groups. Attorney representatives argued that under no-fault motorists would "pay more and receive less" (Brett 1989b). Anticipating the government's eventual support for no-fault, the coalition mounted a public relations campaign against moving away from a tort system even before Elston's announcement. For instance, on 9 August 1989 "concerned members of the Ontario Bar" and others took out a full page advertisement in the (Toronto) *Globe and Mail* proclaiming that: "No Fault Is No Answer in Ontario." The advertisement quoted from the Osborne and OAIB Reports to argue that the government's own studies indicated no-fault would hurt consumers and would not succeed in significantly reducing rates.

After the September announcement, attorneys and their allies stepped up their efforts to incite grass-roots opposition (Mackie 1990). Attorneys made common cause with some advocates for accident victims concerned about the level of benefits under the government's plan (other such groups supported the plan). Letters and columns appeared in newspapers. Opponents made available to public access cable television stations a video attacking no-fault. Some law firms went so far as to write their clients to warn them that they would no longer be able to obtain "pain and suffering" benefits under the government's plan. The attacks on the plan were sufficiently irritating that by January 1990 Elston complained publicly about the "misleading advertising" from a "loose coalition of special interests, directed by a group of personal-injury lawyers" (Mackie 1990).

Leaders of Ontario's other major political parties also attacked OMPP as unfair to consumers and a "sell-out to insurance companies." Peter Kormos, the NDP's flamboyant critic for automobile insurance issues, was a particularly vociferous opponent.[5] Kormos, himself an attorney, spoke out extensively against the plan and in favor of a public automobile insurance system with full tort rights. One legislator I interviewed credited Kormos with pushing the NDP caucus away from simply advocating public ownership, as had traditionally been its stance, and toward championing the unrestricted right to sue for accident losses.

Media commentary on the Liberals' plan was mixed in its assessment. The *Toronto Star*, for instance, provided extensive discussion of options for reforming the automobile insurance system. Immediately following Elston's announcement, a newspaper editorial (1989) provided lukewarm backing of OMPP, endorsing it mainly as an evolutionary step toward the preferred option of a pure no-fault system with public ownership of the industry. Yet at the same time one of the *Star's* columnists blasted the government's plan as a "bizarre idea" for subsidizing the profitable insurance industry as a means of reducing insurance costs (Walkom 1989). The *Star* also ran a series of investigative stories on how no-fault worked in other North American jurisdictions (see for example Walker 1989c). The series was largely critical, emphasizing problems injured motorists faced in obtaining compensation for automobile accidents.

The Progress of the No-Fault Bill

The Liberals' bill to implement the OMPP passed a second reading in the legislature in December of 1989, with the government promising to hold public hearings on the matter. Such hearings were held by a legislative committee in the first two months of 1990. According to one commentator, the legislation "was given exceptionally harsh treatment by health care and legal community lobbyists" (Baetz 1993). Additionally, well-known American consumer advocate Ralph Nader testified against the proposal. As he had in done in many American states such as Rhode Island, Nader condemned no-fault as dehumanizing and a give-away to the insurance industry, calling instead for more stringent regulation (Turner 1990). Opponents at the same time highlighted evidence of grass-roots concern. One of the lead groups against no-fault released the results of a public opinion survey indicating that opposition to the government's no-fault plan outstripped support. Meantime the IBC lobbied in favor of the OMPP, emphasizing especially trial lawyers' financial stake in the tort system, which was said to amount to $500 million annually.

Despite the opposition, the government did not budge. The no-fault plan emerged from the committee hearings essentially intact. In the full legislature the OMPP faced one more hurdle in the form of a filibuster led by Kormos. For almost a full month Kormos tied up action on the bill as he argued that the plan denied fair compensation to accident victims. Kormos also slammed the government plan with

Explaining the Enactment of No-Fault Legislation

exceptionally harsh rhetoric, at one point indicating that "the premier and his gang" were "so deep in the pockets of the [insurance] industry that these guys are spitting out lint" (Monahan 1995, 57). Eventually, the liberals broke the filibuster with a parliamentary maneuver, and the OMPP was approved in a party-line vote in May of 1990. The plan took effect the following month.

EXPLAINING THE ENACTMENT OF NO-FAULT LEGISLATION

After assuming full control of the provincial government following the 1987 election, the Liberals began with an automobile insurance reform strategy that concentrated on rate-making controls. The Liberals then moved to a strategy that focused on restricting tort actions. This latter change was hardly a foregone conclusion; prior to introduction of the OMPP, some commentators explicitly doubted that it would occur (see especially Atkinson and Nigol 1989). How best can we account for the altered approach? That is the critical question considered in this section.

Once again, there is little evidence to support the sufficiency of a pressure theory explanation. Consider the following points:

- During this whole period the message sent to politicians by motorists was both abundantly clear and invariant: find a means of reducing premiums. True, the salience of the automobile insurance issue for drivers varied with the rate of premium growth. Yet there is no reason to think the issue was less salient for motorists in 1987 (following a period of especially rapid premium growth) than in 1989 (when, as indicated earlier, rates had been kept lower by government fiat). Accordingly, there is no rationale to believe that governmental decisions were more "traceable" in 1989 than they had been earlier.
- The insurance companies' position also remained unchanged. Throughout the 1980s the companies, through the IBC, actively supported strong no-fault laws. Moreover, the anecdotal evidence of the increasingly poor public image of insurance companies (undoubtedly as a result of anger over rates) suggests that, if anything, their support paid declining political dividends to politicians. (On the poor image of the insurance companies, see especially Feldthusen 1990.)
- Attorney groups remained constant in their strong opposition to restrictions on tort actions.
- There is no indication that the perceived size of the major groups (and hence their importance in any electoral coalition) varied significantly from the middle to the late 1980s.[6]

- And of course there was no change in the ruling party and hence no change in general core constituency support for governmental policy actions.

On the other hand, there are a number of reasons to believe that between 1987 and 1989 there was a growing Liberal Party consensus (at least among the leadership) about the accuracy of the Pogo Story. At the same time, the Liberals gained a deeper understanding of the various policy instruments consistent with that account. This understanding prompted the Liberals to choose the strong verbal threshold no-fault plan as the most promising option for meeting their goals.

The evidence for this argument comes in a variety of forms. First, my interviews and previous case studies suggest that neither political leaders nor staff for the key ministry (financial institutions) were very knowledgeable about automobile insurance when the rates problem came to the forefront in the middle of the 1980s. In part this was likely the result of the "hands off" regulatory regime in effect at that time. An additional factor may have been the very limited industry efforts at political education; the insurance industry was commonly portrayed as complacent (see especially Atkinson and Nigol 1989). It is therefore reasonable to believe that government officials had not yet settled upon a diagnosis of the nature of the "insurance problem." In the crisis atmosphere that prevailed in 1987, the relatively simple option of moving to impose a rate freeze and tighten regulation likely was quite attractive, even if political leaders were not convinced of its prospects for long-term success. As Bruce Feldthusen (1990, 299) writes:

> In the short run the [Liberal government in April 1987] took the most drastic option available, proposing to freeze premiums as of that date, and to roll back premiums approximately 10 per cent for young males and taxis. This was an attractive pre-election strategy because it conveyed immediately visible and real (if temporary) benefits to a large number of perceived marginal voters. Blunt regulatory initiatives of this type are useful because the perceived benefits are highly visible and easily grasped by the electorate. In contrast, the costs are dispersed and hidden in technical analysis.

Indeed, a key official under the Liberal government acknowledged that the 1987 decisions were made "without much detailed thinking about alternatives" and with an eye toward "buying time" for further consideration of policy options.

Second, during the period studied, Liberal leaders engaged in an extensive effort to educate themselves about automobile insurance. The

Explaining the Enactment of No-Fault Legislation 101

lengthy OAIB hearings were only the most visible, and likely not the most important, source of learning. As noted previously, potentially more important were the regular, closed-door meetings involving top party officials and aimed at examining policy options. Such an environment provided ample opportunity for sharing of information between agency staff and elected officials. Also, by avoiding the necessity of public posturing, this decision-making forum was especially well designed for developing consensus about the nature of the problem and the type of policy change that was needed.

Third, a combination of visible indicators potentially contributed to the conclusion that the Pogo Story (emphasizing underlying cost factors) was accurate, and that the Profiteering Story was unsatisfactory. Moreover, government leaders apparently were cognizant of these indicators. Thus another official involved in the executive committee discussions listed a number of factors suggesting the industry was truly being squeezed. These included government actuarial studies indicating that automobile insurance actually was being provided at a loss, an increase in the portion of consumers in the residual market (i.e., consumers who were considered excessively "high risk" under company underwriting guidelines), and some signs of companies withdrawing from the Ontario market. As he put it, by early 1989, the government had become convinced that "a full tort system with rates suppressed below market level was not viable." Instead, "costs had to be taken out of the system." Such language is strikingly reminiscent of that used by the Casey administration and its supporters in Pennsylvania.

Fourth, the notion of a move toward consensus about the Pogo Story helps to explain the Liberals' decision not to back a public automobile insurance system, despite some commentators at the time suggesting that such a move was inevitable (see for example Walker 1989a). As indicated in chapter 3, support for a public system fits well with the Profiteering Story, but not the Pogo Story. That is, Liberal leaders were likely unconvinced that a public system would be effective because it did not address the real source of the problem. Since the Liberals (unlike NDP members) did not have an ideological commitment to nationalization, there was no point in taking on the difficult public auto insurance battle.

Fifth, the politics of ideas explanation can account for the Liberals' abandonment of the uniform classification system without ever putting it into place; such abandonment is difficult to explain with pressure theory. A uniform classification system would have required substantial subsidies from drivers in relatively low-risk actuarial categories (e.g., middle-aged drivers) to drivers in high-risk categories (e.g., young drivers). It is reasonable to expect that the former would have been very angry once they received their new premium notices and would have pressured lawmakers accordingly. Yet consumers *never received such notices* (O'Donnell 1991, 10). Instead it is reasonable to conclude that industry data presented to Liberal leaders convinced them that the new system would have unacceptable consequences. Two years previously, government officials, then less educated about automobile insurance, ignored such advice. Comments by long-time industry player Allan O'Donnell (1991, 6) are revealing in this regard.

> [T]he most that the [legislation establishing the OAIB and uniform classification system] could [have] accomplish[ed] [was] to reallocate premiums amongst all policyholders in the province without addressing the [underlying] problem [....] The advice of the Insurance Bureau of Canada and individual insurers to the Government fell on deaf ears; the Government's assumption was that insurers were hiding money and generally cooking the books.

What had changed between 1987 (when the industry's advice was ignored) and 1989 (when it was embraced)? The most plausible explanation is that government officials had come to thoroughly embrace the Pogo Story.

There is also reason to believe that Liberal leaders had become much more sophisticated about what specific type of plan was necessary to "remove costs from the system," and especially about the desirable characteristics of a no-fault system. As noted earlier, different reports had come to different conclusions about the effectiveness of no-fault. Previous academic research stresses the lack of clarity among Ontario officials about no-fault's ability to lower rates (Atkinson and Nigol 1989). Yet while there might have been good cause for uncertainty in 1987, this was less true in 1989 when politicians had been briefed extensively about the details of systems operating in other jurisdictions (e.g., Quebec, Michigan, New York) and could better distinguish the more promising models from the less promising ones.

EPILOGUE: THE NDP AND PUBLIC AUTOMOBILE INSURANCE

I have concentrated upon explaining the most dramatic policy shift occurring in Ontario in recent years. Yet if my explanation has wider applicability, it should be capable of accounting for other decisions as well. For this reason, it is helpful to consider briefly a major choice faced by a subsequent Ontario government. The one to which I refer is the NDP's decision to abandon plans to bring a public automobile insurance system to the province.

Epilogue: The NDP and Public Automobile Insurance

As noted previously, in opposition the NDP had long advocated public automobile insurance. Such advocacy was explicitly grounded in a Profiteering Story-type analysis that attributed the rates problem to the discretionary actions of insurance companies. Thus in an official submission to a commission of inquiry, then NDP leader (and later premier) Bob Rae and insurance critic Mel Swart wrote as follows (see Monahan 1995, 55):

> Ontario's current system of private car insurance is highway robbery. Strong words? Nothing less describes the rate-gouging, the profiteering, and the arrogance of private insurance companies in Ontario . . . . We must replace [that system] with an efficient and affordable driver-owned system.

After their surprise electoral victory, NDP officials confirmed their continued support for a public system. Thus in the November 1990 "Throne Speech" NDP leaders indicated that legislation to create a "driver-owned" system would be introduced the following spring (Ferguson 1990). Yet the NDP did not meet its own self-imposed deadline. By the middle of 1991 opposition to the plan within the NDP cabinet had grown to the point that a decision was made to hold an early September caucus retreat to consider the issue. After a lengthy debate, Premier Rae announced publicly that the government had decided not to proceed with public automobile insurance. Furthermore, in extemporaneous remarks Rae all but closed the door to further consideration of the issue (Monahan 1995, 88). Instead, the NDP later opted to push through legislation expanding no-fault benefits while placing further restrictions on tort actions.

Various explanations have been offered for the NDP's retrenchment on public automobile insurance, which constituted one of the clearest instances of abandonment of a traditional party plank. Many such explanations fall within the rubric of a pressure model of decision making. For example, Thomas Walkom (1994, ch. 5) emphasizes the industry's lobbying campaign and its success at mobilizing employees to protest the potential loss of thousands of jobs under a government takeover.[7] The facts that the industry could show that potential job losers were disproportionately female was seen to be particularly threatening to the NDP, given the party's public commitment to sexual equality.

Yet there is another equally plausible explanation, and one consistent with some actual public and private statements by NDP officials. That explanation is that party officials lost faith in their own professed diagnosis of the nature of the "insurance problem," while confronting the full reality of the costs of a public takeover. The NDP leaders were faced with analyses and estimates from civil servants indicating that "efficiency" savings from a government takeover were at best small, and likely overshadowed by increased costs from restoring the right to sue, as the NDP also had promised to do. Additionally, a number of studies indicated that borrowing the type of money necessary to fund the startup for the new program would be difficult and very costly given Ontario's then bleak economy. According to one high-ranking government official, the government learned it would be "killed" by the bond market if it went ahead with a plan that required $1.4 billion in new capital. Combined with the unemployment issue, these considerations dramatically undermined the attractiveness of the public automobile insurance option.

In his study of the NDP in power, Patrick Monahan essentially offers a similar explanation of the NDP's change of heart, if one laced with more sarcasm and rhetorical flourish. He writes (1995, 61; emphasis in original):

> While in opposition, Bob Rae and Peter Kormos could ignore the fact that auto-insurance rates were going up primarily because payouts to accident victims were skyrocketing. Instead, they could blame rising premiums on company rip-offs or industry gangsters cutting deals with their friends in government. This simplistic view led to an equally simplistic solution: establish a driver-owned auto-insurance system and—*poof!*— overnight, six million drivers would have cheaper insurance. And that wasn't all. The NDP also claimed that their [sic] system would deliver more money to those injured in auto accidents: more generous payments *and* at a cheaper cost. It seemed too good to be true.
>
> Well, of course, it was too good to be true. But talk is cheap, especially for an opposition politician. It is easy to stand on the floor of the legislature and blame the high cost of auto insurance on gangsters and insurance rip-offs. It is quite another to deliver on the promises made in opposition.

In short, there is a plausible explanation for both the Liberal Party's move to embrace no-fault in the late 1980s and the New Democratic Party's decision to abandon public automobile insurance in the 1990s. That explanation focuses upon changes in what politicians believed about the consequences of policy choices.

NOTES TO CHAPTER 6

1. Interview with the author, fall of 1995 (anonymity requested).
2. While adequate for present purposes, it is somewhat simplistic to portray the Ontario political landscape as a battle among parties that can be clearly aligned across a single ideological spectrum. White (1989, 14) has argued that

Notes to Chapter 6

the Liberal and Progressive Conservative Parties "have, in recent decades, both aspired to a moderate, centrist position in the political spectrum." By contrast, the NDP has tended to take more firm ideological positions. Some have argued that this ideological cohesion diminished when the NDP actually governed the province during the first half of the 1990s; see Walkom 1994.

3. Peterson's pledge is widely noted in discussions of the automobile insurance controversy; see for example Walker 1989b.

4. These figures subsequently were revised downward, but only after the original numbers had been widely publicized and stirred public anger.

5. Under Ontario's parliamentary system, a specific member of an opposition party is often designated as the "critic" of the government's policies in a particular subject area. The critic serves as spokesperson for the opposition in that area and commonly has responsibility for cross-examination of ministers during question period.

6. One caveat should be noted, however. It is possible to argue that while the insurance industry's political stance, size, and public image did not change significantly during the late 1980s, its political organization improved. Some of those I interviewed made this claim. To the extent this is true, pressure from the industry may have been somewhat more effective at the end of the decade.

7. Whether in fact the employees were mobilized by industry lobbyists or were "self-mobilized" appears to be a matter of some controversy; Monahan (1995) offers the latter interpretation.

7

The Parliamentary System Difference

> For politicians seeking to impose losses on powerful groups, the structure of institutions matters[.]
> —Paul D. Pierson and R. Kent Weaver (1993, 150)

To this point, I have emphasized the importance of the politics of ideas and the nature of the causal story about automobile insurance reform elected officials tend to accept. Institutional differences are another crucial consideration in explaining varying policy decisions. One is easily struck by Ontario's more ready embrace of (multiple) reforms than was the case in *either* Pennsylvania or Rhode Island. In this chapter I will argue that the apparent difference between parliamentary and separation-of-powers systems is not limited to the above jurisdictions. Rather, there is evidence of general policy divergence between the American states and Canadian provinces. That is, the provinces' Westminster parliamentary systems made it easier to adopt far-reaching reforms, as well as to reverse such reforms when party leaders' problem diagnosis shifted.[1]

In addition to the previous case studies, I will draw upon two other sources of information. First, I will use aggregate data about policy decisions in all fifty American states and ten Canadian provinces. Second, I will draw upon "mini-case studies" of policy decisions in two additional Canadian provinces (Manitoba and Saskatchewan) and one additional American state (Hawaii). The cases were not randomly selected, but rather chosen with an eye toward what they suggest about institutional differences.

Before presenting the empirical evidence, it is necessary to consider the nature of the argument about how institutions matter in somewhat more depth. I do so in the following section, stressing the ability to impose losses on powerful groups.

LOSS IMPOSITION AND GOVERNMENTAL SYSTEM DIFFERENCES

The ability to impose losses is the key to how governmental system differences affect automobile insurance public policy decisions. If it

106

works as planned, significant automobile insurance reform creates winners, most notably among the mass driving public. Yet such reform also creates losers, be they trial lawyers, insurance companies, medical providers, and/or at least some insurance consumers themselves. As has been shown, groups facing such losses strenuously resist them. Additionally, policymakers may be uncertain about what they are really buying by "taking on" trial lawyers or other groups.

Previous research suggests that governmental system differences may influence the ability to imposes losses. The multination study by Weaver, Bert A. Rockman, and their colleagues is especially notable in this regard (see especially Pierson and Weaver 1993; Weaver and Rockman 1993b). Weaver and Rockman conclude that while the effects of constitutional arrangements are not unidirectional, separation-of-powers systems provide significantly greater-than-average risk of failure to impose losses when needed to serve some larger public purpose (e.g., deficit reduction). By contrast, they find that parliamentary systems, especially the "party government" type systems dominant in countries such as Canada, provide greater opportunities for loss imposition. The major factors contributing to the advantages of the parliamentary system are the lesser number of veto points loss-imposition proposals must face and the greater cohesiveness of political parties (making it difficult for interest groups to "pick off" individual legislators).

The no-fault battles in Rhode Island and Ontario are illustrative of how the above factors may work. In Rhode Island, neither the backing of a Democratic administration nor the overwhelming Democratic majority in the state legislature prevented the need to stitch together a coalition of individual lawmakers. As I have shown, rank-and-file lawyer-lawmakers from both parties formed a solid bulwark of opposition to abandoning traditional tort. Even legislators without a tie to traditional no-fault opponents had to be convinced that no-fault would work. This was a difficult task, especially in an environment in which a variety of groups (including Ocean State Action with its claim to pursuit of the "public interest") were arguing on behalf of the Profiteering Story. By contrast, in Ontario a small group of Liberal Party leaders developed the plan to reform the automobile insurance system. Much of the important policy debate occurred outside the public view, although with considerable outside information and consultation. There was some grumbling among Liberal back-benchers about lack of involvement, given the plan's significance and the strenuous opposition it engendered. Yet as is typical under a parliamentary system, the backbenchers supported their leaders' position once it had been announced. Neither the vigorous opposition of attorney groups and their allies nor the professional sympathies of the large number of lawyers in the caucus were sufficient to alter the Liberal Party's stance.[2]

While a strong intuitive case can be made for the superiority of Westminster parliamentary systems for loss imposition, the existence of such an advantage in the real world is an empirical question rather than a logical inevitability. A skeptic might doubt the advantage for a number of reasons, including the following:

- As Weaver and Pierson emphasize, the greater concentration of accountability focused on leaders under the Westminster system might make them relatively more nervous about taking the blame for losses. By contrast, the diffuse accountability of separation of powers might actually ease loss imposition.
- Competition between branches and parties under a separation-of-powers system might lead to a "bidding up" process whereby potential losses for some are increased in an effort to be more ambitious about meeting the needs of others.[3]
- Institutional differences might simply be overwhelmed by other factors. In an analogous argument, David R. Mayhew (1991) finds that the difference between divided and unified government has little impact on the amount of major legislation enacted by the American national government; factors such as long term-trends in public opinion are much more significant.

For these reasons, it is important that the conclusion reached by Weaver and Rockman is based on empirical evidence, rather than theory alone. Yet it is also necessary to appreciate the tentativeness of their arguments; they write (1993b, 455) of the advantage of Westminster systems "probably [being] stronger on average" than the disadvantage. Such caution is justified given that the supporting data are somewhat thin. All the empirical information for their work comes from national-level case studies involving a small number of countries. Accordingly, there is the need for the further confirmation that can be provided by analysis of a larger number of jurisdictions in a different context. That is what I aim to offer.

THE STATES AND THE PROVINCES: AGGREGATE ANALYSIS

To provide a more thorough test of the argument that Canada's parliamentary system made it easier to impose losses, I focus on the question of whether jurisdictions adopted no-fault insurance laws between

The States and the Provinces: Aggregate Analysis 109

1 January 1990 and 30 June 1995. Again, this was a period in which rising insurance rates commonly emerged as a salient issue for the mass public in both countries. There are three reasons why I concentrate on the no-fault reform option. First, legislative action is required to impose no-fault, thereby making national institutional differences relevant in a way they might not be if reforms could be adopted by administrative action alone. Second, complete information is available on the automobile accident recovery systems operating in all states and provinces and any recent changes that have been made. Third, no-fault probably has been the most common proposal for major change to automobile insurance systems on both sides of the forty-ninth parallel.

In table 7.1 I classify all American states and Canadian provinces (using their commonly recognized postal codes) in terms of their automobile insurance systems and show changes that occurred in the first part of the 1990s.[4] The categories are arranged in order of the degree to which lawsuits are restricted. "Traditional tort systems" do not limit legal action in any manner. "Monetary threshold no-fault systems" allow lawsuits only if injured parties' medical losses exceed a specified dollar amount. These systems are generally seen to provide weak restrictions on legal actions. "Verbal threshold no-fault systems" limit lawsuits for some types of compensation (and in some versions, limit all lawsuits) to instances in which accident victims have suffered specified injuries such as permanent disfigurement. Such systems are commonly viewed as more effective in reducing litigation and lowering costs. Finally, "pure no-fault systems" bar all lawsuits. I refer to the last two types of systems as "strong no-fault systems."

To highlight the information from table 7.1 most relevant to my central argument, in table 7.2 I summarize the patterns with respect to loss imposition. As shown in table 7.2, during the period I studied, three of ten Canadian provinces imposed the losses necessitated by a move to a no-fault system, or from an existing no-fault system to a stronger one. Manitoba and Saskatchewan moved all the way to pure no-fault, while Ontario adopted a verbal threshold system. Among the American states, only Pennsylvania adopted any sort of no-fault and, as has been shown, that was a "choice system." Furthermore, two states (Connecticut and Georgia) moved to weaken limits on tort action; no provinces did so.

In short, a review of the legal status of no-fault insurance in all subnational jurisdictions tends to support the original claim about the importance of institutional differences. It indeed appears to have been easier for the Canadian parliamentary governments to impose the types of losses necessitated by no-fault.

TABLE 7.1.
Change and Continuity in American and Canadian Insurance Systems, 1990–1995 (Canadian provinces in bold; strong no-fault systems in italics)

Insurance System as of 1 January 1990	Traditional Tort	Monetary Threshold No-Fault	Verbal Threshold No-Fault	Pure No-Fault
	Insurance System as of 1 July 1995*			
Traditional Tort	AL, AK, AZ, AR, CA, DE, ID, IL, IN, IO, LA, ME, MD, MS, MO, MT, NE, NV, NH, NM, NC, OH, OK, OR, RI, SC, SD, TN, TX, VT, VA, WA, WV, WI, WY	(none)	PA[1] ——— **ON**	(no states) ——— ***MB, SK***
	AB, BC, NB, NF, NS, PE			
Monetary Threshold No-Fault	CT, GA ——— (no provinces)	CO, HI, KS, KY, MA, MN, ND, UT	(none)	(none)
Verbal Threshold No-Fault	(none)	(none)	FL, MI, NJ, NY	(none)
Pure No-Fault	(none)	(none)	(none)	(no states) ——— ***PQ***

*New Jersey and Pennsylvania had "choice" no-fault systems as of 1 July 1995 (that is, consumers could opt for traditional tort or no-fault coverage, subject to a verbal threshold). Kentucky had a "choice" system with a monetary threshold.

TABLE 7.2.
Summary of Loss Imposing Moves during the Early 1990s (percentages in brackets)

	Canadian Provinces	American States
Jurisdictions Imposing Losses Necessitated by No-Fault	3 [30]	1 [2]
Jurisdictions Making No Change	7 [70]	47 [94]
Jurisdictions Reversing No-Fault Losses	0 [0]	2 [4]

MINI-CASE STUDIES: MANITOBA, SASKATCHEWAN, AND HAWAII

Aggregate analysis does not illuminate further the means by which institutional differences may affect public policy choices. Such mechanisms can be seen by a brief review of what transpired in a few jurisdictions. Below I examine events in Manitoba and Saskatchewan, where pure no-fault laws were enacted, and Hawaii, where among all American states there was the closest thing to a "near-miss" with respect to adopting pure no-fault.

Manitoba

The striking thing about Manitoba was how quickly elite consensus about necessary policy action was translated into a major overhaul of the automobile insurance system. The Progressive Conservative Party government came to power in 1988 in part because of public dissatisfaction with how the previous NDP government had handled the automobile insurance issue.[5] However, the Progressive Conservatives did not have a platform calling for enactment of no-fault and in fact traditionally had supported the tort recovery system (thereby enjoying good relations with the trial lawyers).[6] As late as the spring of 1992 the government had expressed official skepticism about no-fault. This was illustrated well in the following legislative committee exchange between Leonard Evans, an NDP member of the provincial legislature, and Glen Cummings, the minister with responsibility for administering the Manitoba Public Insurance Corporation Act.[7]

> *Evans.* [W]hat is happening to no-fault insurance? Are we moving in that direction? Is that a possibility, or is that totally out of the question?
> *Cummings.* [. . .] I have continually said that we are not dispensing of any ways or means that might be used to improve delivery of service to the driving public, but I have to say that there is no initiative afoot or no desire on my part at this point to move to no-fault insurance[. . . .] When you compare our insurance costs with other costs across the country and when you compare our benefits with no-fault, when you compare the costs to society, I still have not seen the proof that I would need to see to move in [the no-fault] direction and to take away from the aggrieved party the right to further compensation[.]

Yet barely more than a year later the government announced support for a pure no-fault system modeled after that operating in Quebec. What had changed? The answer is not anything significant in the interest-group environment. Rather by all accounts (including those of some people opposed to pure no-fault), the key factor was new information from the Manitoba Public Insurance Corporation (MPIC) indicating that in the absence of major changes automobile insurance rates were projected to as much as double by the turn of the century. The projected increases was attributed to a sharp rise in the total costs of personal injury claims (see also figure 3.2). According to the MPIC, costs associated with lawsuits for minor accidents were an especially significant part of the rise in claims costs.[8] Faced with the MPIC data, Cummings became convinced that existing government plans to control costs (e.g., by enhancing automobile safety) were not sufficient.[9] After considering a number of no-fault models, Cummings decided that a Quebec-type system would likely work best and recommended such a plan to the cabinet. The cabinet accepted the recommendation, and the government announced the plan in May of 1993.

Attorney groups, already on record as being opposed to no-fault, vehemently opposed the government's plan, although they appear to have been slow to organize because of doubts that a Progressive Conservative regime would move in that direction.[10] Lawyers claimed that the new system would do great harm to many accident victims, who would be denied full compensation for their injuries. Attorneys also offered their own cost-cutting alternatives. But this opposition was to no avail. Party rank-and-file assented, and a mere two months later final legislative approval was granted to a plan that completely barred access to the tort system for damages related to automobile accidents.[11]

In summary, we see further evidence of how the capacity for top-down, executive-centered decision making under Westminster systems empowers governments to impose the types of losses necessitated by major automobile insurance reform. Consistent with the caveats offered

Mini-Case Studies: Manitoba, Saskatchewan, and Hawaii 113

by Weaver and Rockman, one might have guessed that the accountability of party government would have checked the willingness of Progressive Conservative Party leaders to commit to a specific plan. However, any such reluctance was overshadowed by the ease with which executive consensus was translated into a policy choice. Once the relevant minister was convinced of the need for no-fault, the path to legislative enactment was neither bumpy nor long. And the concerns expressed by lawyers were brushed aside.

Saskatchewan

Events in Saskatchewan largely reinforce the main lesson from Manitoba, hence I will review them more briefly. Saskatchewan's NDP government of the early 1990s—nominally if not in fact a government of the left—had been elected without a mandate to adopt no-fault.[12] Sharp increases in injury claims costs led to fiscal pressures on the public automobile insurance system, prompting government leaders to consider major system changes.[13] The public insurance corporation commissioned a 1993 study of the current system by an actuarial firm, which in large part attributed rising claims costs to increasing costs of lawsuits. The study examined a number of policy options but recommended adoption of a pure no-fault system (Sobeco Ernst & Young 1993). The government insurance corporation in turn backed the plan, and the provincial cabinet did so as well. In April 1994 the responsible minister announced the plan publicly, and in the following month implementing legislation was enacted into law.

For my purposes, the most striking feature of the adoption of no-fault in Saskatchewan was that the lawyers were well organized. The earlier enactment of no-fault in Manitoba helped to mobilize Saskatchewan attorneys who anticipated that a similar effort might be forthcoming in their province. Indeed, many of the tactics used by provincial attorneys were the same as those used by American lawyers opposed to no-fault, as well as by attorney groups in Ontario. Representatives of the Saskatchewan Trial Lawyers Association met privately with the responsible minister on multiple occasions, sent letters to each NDP legislator, and urged members to contact their own representatives (Wyatt 1994). A media campaign was conducted, involving full-page advertisements in local papers, appearances on radio and television shows, submission of letters-to-the-editor critical of no-fault, issuing of press releases, and tactics of that sort.[14] Attempts were made to enlist other groups as allies, although trial lawyer representatives acknowledged that such efforts were less successful than they had hoped. Simply put, lawyers made a major effort in Saskatchewan. Yet the government was determined to move on no-fault, and only minor changes were made to the NDP proposal.

Hawaii

As noted earlier, one can imagine a scenario in which the separation-of-powers system actually encourages loss imposition through a kind of "bidding up" process. Under this scenario, a policy actor (or set of policy actors) in one branch offers a proposal aimed at providing broad benefits (e.g., a strengthened economy as the result of deficit reduction), but also necessitating major losses. Motivated by institutional rivalry, public relations, or other considerations, a policy actor(s) in the other branch responds by making a proposal that purports to offer even more widespread benefits, the costs for which is imposing still deeper losses on some people. The result is that decision makers are led to support a proposal for more radical change than was originally envisioned by actors in either branch.

The difficulty with this scenario is that it assumes that divergent policy actors will find the same tradeoff (e.g., more deficit reduction for further program reductions) compelling, once it has been publicized. Yet not only may decision makers from different branches value the tradeoff differently, but they may disagree on the probability that the benefits of loss imposition will in fact be realized. For instance, legislators might doubt that reducing the deficit will have the salutary economic consequences envisioned by an elected executive. If this is the case, the multiple veto points and weak party discipline of the American system may strengthen the hand of those opposed to the losses.

This brings us to the Hawaiian case.[15] Automobile insurance had long been a major, controversial issue in that state, as a consequence of the especially high rates paid by Hawaiian drivers (calculated to be on average the highest in the United States in 1992).[16] Hawaii operated under a monetary threshold no-fault system, which even no-fault advocates acknowledged at best to be ineffective in limiting premium hikes. Earlier reform efforts were widely perceived as having failed, and consideration of further reforms figured prominently in the 1994 election campaign.

Democrat Benjamin Cayetano, an attorney by trade, took office as the state's new governor at the beginning of 1995. He proposed (1) eliminating no-fault, thereby restoring full tort rights and (2) replacing the existing first party no-fault benefits with a requirement that the state's mandatory employer health plan coverage be extended to cover automobile accident injuries. (An estimated 97 percent of Hawaiians were covered by the state's unique, mandatory employer health cover-

Alternative Explanations

age law; see Botticelli 1995.) The health plan mandate in effect implied that the state's businesses would have to take a loss, since they would face higher health insurance costs. The administration claimed that such a move would result in major overall consumer savings because responsibility for paying automobile insurance losses would be more widely distributed, since many drivers were currently uninsured. Critics contended that the plan would simply lead to cost shifting.

Lawmakers responded in a manner that initially seemed consistent with the "bidding up" scenario. While Democrats dominated both houses of the state legislature, rivalry between legislative leaders and the governor of the same party was commonly acknowledged. Faced with the governor's plan, a senate committee chair offered a radical alternative. Essentially, the legislator borrowed the governor's idea of paying for auto injuries through employer health insurance and combined that with the idea of moving to pure no-fault. Such a massive change in the auto insurance system was to make possible elimination of the requirement that motorists carry insurance, elimination of bodily injury liability insurance entirely, and average premium reductions of 45 percent or more.[17] Politically the implication was that losses to businesses were to be reduced somewhat relative to the Cayetano plan, attorneys were to take a big hit, accident victims were to have their legal options severely limited, and even insurance companies might suffer lost revenue—all in the name of providing windfall premium savings to the average consumer. The plan was attractive enough to secure passage in the State Senate; eventually the House of Representatives followed suit.

But in the end the separation of powers allowed for torpedoing even that rare American strong no-fault plan that achieved legislative approval. After the pure no-fault bill was passed by the legislature, trial attorneys, some insurance companies, and some consumer advocates (notably Ralph Nader and his allies) urged Cayetano to veto the measure, which he did.[18] The governor himself apparently never warmed to the notion of restricting lawsuits. In his veto message, Cayetano argued that the bill was likely to be found unconstitutional, that the benefits were questionable, and that people who had suffered great harm would unfairly be barred access to tort remedies.[19] Thus after a tumultuous battle, the status quo was preserved.

ALTERNATIVE EXPLANATIONS

Evidence presented thus far supports the hypothesis that the Canadian parliamentary system made it easier to impose the losses necessitated by automobile insurance reform. Yet alternative explanations exist for the different patterns across the forty-ninth parallel. Before concluding my argument, such explanations need to be considered in more depth.

One alternative explanation is that differences in the strength of attorney interests account for variant outcomes across the two countries. This account cannot be completely rejected. The litigiousness of American society is commonly emphasized, as is the large number of lawyers within and outside of government (see especially Miller 1995). In this regard it is important to note that there were slightly over three attorneys for every one thousand people in the United States in 1990, while no Canadian province had as many as two attorneys for every one thousand people.[20]

If attorney strength is to be taken seriously as an alternative explanation, such differences in the *size* of the potential attorney lobby seemingly would need to be critical. As shown in this and earlier chapters, there is no appreciable difference across the two countries in the consistency of lawyers' opposition to no-fault as a means of automobile insurance reform, the intensity of that opposition, or the nature of the arguments made by attorneys. There are even similarities in many of the tactics used (e.g., forging alliances with consumer groups, conducting media campaigns). Moreover, some of the differences between the role of lawyers in the two countries are endogenous to the system of government. For example, lawyers traditionally have dominated judiciary committees in American legislatures, to which tort-reform measures may be referred (Miller 1995). Yet such dominance is only significant in a system that grants substantial deference to legislative committees.

A second possibility is that the existence of public automobile insurance systems makes it easier to adopt no-fault. This argument also cannot be dismissed, although it seems less plausible. As shown, two of the three Canadian provinces that adopted no-fault earlier in the decade (Manitoba and Saskatchewan) had public systems. It might be contended that the government's role in insurance provision places an especially large burden on politicians for ensuring rate stability, since consumers will view premiums as a virtual tax. Additionally, it might be argued that clear, consistent pro-reform messages from the public insurance corporations were critical to the actual adoption of reform plans.

However, there are the following four problems with the public automobile insurance alternative argument. (1) Even in jurisdictions where insurance is supplied by private firms, increases in premiums are commonly viewed as a virtual tax, given the prevailing legal mandate that consumers carry at least liability insurance (a point discussed at more length in chapter 3). (2) Private-sector insurance industries in both countries, while notoriously fractious, have also managed to offer quite consistent support for no-fault. In some cases, such as the 1993 battle in Rhode Island, companies have devoted extensive resources to the no-fault cause. (3) Ontario remains prominent as a jurisdiction in which different automobile insurance reform measures were adopted without backing from a public corporation. (4) It is quite likely that the move to public automobile insurance is itself endogenous to the existence of a parliamentary system. Thus Manitoba's adoption of public automobile insurance required a hard-fought battle and a high level of cohesiveness by members of the NDP advocating the change.[21] It seems doubtful that such an effort would have been successful in the United States.

A third alternative explanation holds that country-specific patterns of policy diffusion might account for the divergent outcomes. That is, other Canadian provinces—but not the American states—looked toward Quebec's success at holding down rates with its pure no-fault system. Some research in other areas suggests that Americans tend either to be oblivious of Canadian policy models, or to exaggerate the problems of transferring lessons from Canada across the border.[22] And anecdotal evidence suggests that governmental officials in Canada were indeed relatively more conscious of the Quebec insurance experience. However, the diffusion argument is weakened by the facts that American models of strong no-fault systems existed before the period I studied, and that these models were widely discussed. For example, the Rhode Island proposal was explicitly modeled after New York's verbal threshold system.

In short, while the alternative explanations cannot be dismissed, none seems to provide a compelling case against the argument that institutional differences help account for the varying outcomes across the two countries. Major automobile insurance reform is difficult to achieve in part because it prompts strong opposition. My analysis suggests that such opposition is easier to overcome under a Westminster-style parliamentary system.

NOTES TO CHAPTER 7

1. For an earlier version of this argument, see Lascher 1998.
2. Over 20 percent of the members of the Liberal caucus (and a virtually identical portion of all Ontario lawmakers) were attorneys, a proportion that was actually higher than the average proportion of attorneys in American state legislatures in 1986. My calculations are based on information in *Canadian Parliamentary Guide* 1989 and Squire 1992.
3. Weaver and Rockman (1993b, 451–52) make a similar argument with respect to how divided government may encourage policy innovation through a "bidding up" process.

4. The classification scheme is based on a) Joost 1992 and b) my 1995 survey of insurance officials.

5. The public's dissatisfaction with the NDP over the insurance issue was underscored by a report prepared by Provincial Judge Robert L. Kopstein in 1988. The NDP government itself commissioned the study, which was aimed at determining how the MPIC could provide "low cost, high quality automobile insurance on a self-sustaining basis." Based on public hearings at a number of locales, Kopstein (1988, part II, 2) concluded as follows: "People felt deceived and betrayed by a perception that facts relating to MPIC's financial condition had been withheld from them. They blamed the sharp rate increases in 1988 premiums upon unwarranted government interference aimed at keeping the rates artificially low, in preceding years, to political advantage[....] Virtually in unison, [those who testified] indicated they were upset by the shock of [a] sudden, sharp [rate] increase."

6. Interviews with people knowledgeable about automobile insurance politics and public policy in Manitoba. See also Bilinkoff 1993.

7. I am grateful to Leonard Evans for providing me the 18 April 1992 transcript of the hearing by the Standing Committee on Public Utilities and Natural Resources that included this exchange.

8. For a summary of the relevant data analysis, see MPIC 1993. For further support of the political importance of the MPIC recommendation, see also the *Winnipeg Free Press* 1993. It should be noted that in emphasizing the pivotal role of rising tort costs, the MPIC study essentially echoed the conclusions of the Kopstein report.

9. Telephone interview with Minister Cummings, 1 June 1995.

10. The Manitoba Bar Association (1989) developed a lengthy report in response to Kopstein's study, which had recommended adoption of a pure no-fault system. In that report the MBA took issue with Kopstein's claims about the ill effects of the tort system and argued that estimated savings under the proposed no-fault plan were overstated.

11. Interestingly, the opposition NDP caucus supported the government's plan based on its earlier commitment to no-fault, although this position generated significant debate within that caucus. Within the provincial legislature itself only the small Liberal Party caucus opposed the plan.

12. Indeed, critics scored the NDP government for failing to engage in adequate debate about no-fault prior to introduction of legislation in the spring of 1994. For example, during question period an opposition lawmaker argued: "No-fault insurance was not an issue in the 1991 election. It was not even mentioned in the throne speech [outlining the government's legislative agenda];" quoted in Mandryk 1994a; see also Mandryk 1994b.

13. On the significance of the losses suffered by the public automobile insurance agency, see for example Wyatt 1994.

14. July 1995 correspondence and materials provided me by J. Duane Koch, a Regina attorney active in the campaign against the government-proposed no-fault legislation.

15. My analysis of the Hawaii case is based largely on the work of my then research assistant, Matthew Newman, who gathered most of the relevant materials, interviewed Hawaiian policy actors, and provided me with a sum-

Notes to Chapter 7

mary analysis of what had transpired in 1995. I am grateful to Matt for his fine work.

16. For an overview of the automobile insurance issue in Hawaii in the middle of the 1990s, see Sullivan 1994; see also Daysog 1995.

17. For a more complete description of the plan proposed by Senate Consumer Protection Committee chairman Milton Holt, see the *Honolulu Advertiser* 1995.

18. Contrary to some claims that the pure no-fault plan was an insurance industry ploy, that proposal was in fact controversial within the ranks of insurance companies. Firms apparently recognized that they might well lose money under the new plan, because net profits might fall (as the result of sharply reduced overall revenues) even if profit margins rose. Thus State Farm Insurance appears to have been virtually alone in taking a "principled" stand in support of the no-fault proposal. See especially Sullivan 1996.

19. Governor Benjamin J. Cayetano, "Statement of Objections to Senate Bill No. 1762, S.D. 1, H.D. 1, C.D. 1," 20 June 1995.

20. Sources for this information include Statistics Canada and NAIC 1993.

21. Brian E. Owen, president of Western Opinion Research, Inc., and author of a dissertation on the adoption of a public automobile insurance system in Manitoba.

22. See for example Marmor 1993. On the other hand, Barry G. Rabe (1994, 26) argues it is common for environmental policy ideas to be diffused in both directions across the American-Canadian national boundary.

8

Conclusion: Learning from Automobile Insurance Reform

In the recent past, many American states and Canadian provinces faced a common problem: high and/or rapidly rising automobile insurance rates. Responses to this problem varied greatly both across jurisdictions and over time. Some subnational governments made only incremental changes. Others (e.g., Hawaii) flirted with major changes but essentially preserved the status quo. Still others (e.g., Pennsylvania, Manitoba) adopted major reforms. And Ontario was notable for moving in different directions during a single party's administration of the provincial government.

I have attempted to explain the different policy choices, and in so doing make more general arguments about key factors that influence policy decisions. In this chapter I summarize the main arguments and draw implications for other issues.

1. *Differences in policymakers' beliefs about the potential effectiveness of automobile insurance reforms partly explain variance in policy choices.* Why was choice no-fault enacted in Pennsylvania and not in Rhode Island? Why did Pennsylvania lawmakers first embrace a premium reduction proposal that did not require limits on tort action and then abandon that plan in favor of a proposal that challenged both legal and medical interests? Why did party leaders in Ontario initially embrace tight regulation and then move toward strong no-fault? Why did a Manitoba government with strong trial-lawyer ties adopt a proposal prohibiting use of the court system for automobile accident claims? It is difficult to answer these questions without reference to decision makers' beliefs about the likely consequences of their actions. Automobile insurance reform is tough; if it is to be adopted, large groups of identifiable people will suffer major, tangible losses. Moreover, some sorts of reforms are tougher than others. Policymakers may be willing to accept the required losses, but only if they are convinced that a plan has a high probability of working and that there is no "easier" way (i.e., a feasible alternative that imposes fewer losses) to provide the rate relief consumers desire.

If my argument is accurate, attention needs to be directed toward a number of issues that are not emphasized by even sophisticated

Conclusion: Learning from Automobile Insurance Reform 121

versions of pressure theory. Among these issues are the coherence and credibility of the causal information provided decision makers and the extent to which such information resonates with what politicians take as established facts. Such events as the rare 1990 victory for comprehensive automobile insurance reform in Pennsylvania can be attributed in part to the compelling nature of the case made for the likelihood of success.

I do not wish to discount the likelihood of either rationalization or cognitive error. One need not be a cynic to find it more than coincidental that Rhode Island's lawyer-legislators (whose expertise would seem to lie elsewhere than analyzing insurance markets) all tended to conclude that the automobile insurance industry was monopolistic and that no-fault had failed to reduce premium hikes in other states. Such views ran sharply against those of people who study insurance markets for a living (see Lascher and Powers 1997). However, the existence of some degree of rationalization and cognitive error does not imply that judgments about policy consequences are irrelevant, or simply byproducts of decisions made for other reasons.

2. *Policymakers' views about policy consequences were embedded in causal stories.* My research highlights the importance of stories about the nature of the "insurance problem." Specifically, I contend that two stories were common: a) one that attributed rate concerns to exploitation of the consumer public by insurance companies (the Profiteering Story); and b) another that attributed rate concerns to rising claims costs, for which consumers themselves were partially responsible (the Pogo Story). Acceptance of one of these stories implied conclusions about what public policy options would work. Accordingly, such acceptance pushed decision makers toward some policy solutions and away from others.

In a world where such stories matter, policy change is in part a matter of decision makers moving to consensus about a particular story. I contend that this is what occurred in Ontario during the latter part of the 1980s. Over time Liberal Party leaders moved toward consensus about the Pogo Story; it fit the information provided them and the accumulating evidence from the province's experiment with tight regulation. Once such consensus was reached, the Liberals' embrace of some form of strong no-fault followed naturally.

The changing sentiment within the ranks of Ontario's Liberal Party underscores another point: acceptance of one or another story was not "hard-wired" by party ideology. Those on the left may have more readily attributed the rates problem to the action of insurance companies, while those on the right may have been more inclined to reject these notions, but these were at most tendencies. In this regard, it is important to reemphasize the following points.

122 Conclusion: Learning from Automobile Insurance Reform

- Pennsylvania's Governor Casey, a Democrat, clearly articulated a Pogo Story explanation of the nature of the insurance problem then facing the state. The governor's Republican (e.g., Representative Freind) and Democratic (e.g., Representative Hayden) allies in the House offered similar explanations.
- There was a substantial amount of bipartisan support for no-fault proposals among rank-and-file state legislators in Pennsylvania and Rhode Island, as well as a substantial amount of bipartisan opposition.
- Some Canadian ministers charged with responsibility for automobile insurance regulation, and hailing from different political parties, expressed similar views about the nature of the insurance problem.
- Strong no-fault systems were adopted in three provinces led by governments of ideologically dissimilar political parties (i.e., the Liberal Party in Ontario, the Progressive Conservative Party in Manitoba, and the NDP in Saskatchewan).
- No-fault proposals were rejected by an ideologically diverse set of American state legislatures.

3. *The Westminster parliamentary system made it easier to impose the losses necessitated by major automobile insurance reform.* There is striking variance in policy choices across the forty-ninth parallel. I contend that the differences are traceable in significant part to institutional divergence. The Canadian provinces' Westminster parliamentary system appears to have made it easier to impose necessary losses than did the American states' separation-of-powers system.

My institutional argument is complementary to my argument about the importance of beliefs about policy consequences. In both Canada and the United States, it mattered whether decision makers embraced a particular story about the insurance problem. However, institutional differences affected the size of the decision-making group that needed to reach story consensus and the ease with which consensus was translated into an actual policy choice.

BEYOND AUTOMOBILE INSURANCE REFORM

If there is an overriding message for political scientists it might be summarized as follows: pay more attention to the stories decision makers tell about the nature of the problems they are asked to address. Such stories may be lacking in subtlety. They may well be "borrowed" from interested parties (and in any event, it is likely that they were articulated first by people other than elected officials themselves). But

Beyond Automobile Insurance Reform

if my argument is correct, the stories politicians tell nevertheless *make a difference* with respect to the actual decisions that are made. Furthermore, politicians are not unyielding in their embrace of particular stories, although change may come slowly. This implies the possibility of altering policy choices by changing the stories that are believed.

Certainly we would expect that changing story acceptance is much easier in some areas than others. There are two reasons to hypothesize that politicians more readily embrace different stories about automobile insurance reform than about many other matters. First, battles over automobile insurance reform tend to center around the best means of solving a commonly recognized problem, and do not generally tap core value conflicts among legislators (with the notable exception of lawyer-legislators, for whom preservation of tort rights may constitute a core value). By contrast, views about the nature of the "welfare problem" tend to correlate highly with the fundamental ideological divisions between political parties. This makes it especially difficult for politicians to alter the stories they accept, since these stories are consistently reinforced by party colleagues and electoral support coalitions (see Kennedy 1987).

Second, in the automobile insurance arena, politicians may be seen to have an unusually strong incentive to "get the story right." It will be readily apparent if reforms are enacted but rates continue to rise. If rates fail to rise but carriers drop their automobile insurance lines or take similar actions, many people will notice. Obviously public monitoring of policy outcomes will be far from perfect, but it is likely to be better in the area of automobile insurance than in many others.

This does not imply that there will be story convergence. Feedback occurs, and this affects what politicians believe. But perceived problems may fade before the feedback makes much difference. Returning to automobile insurance reform, it is notable that throughout the United States, rate increases diminished by the middle of the 1990s, for reasons unrelated to the reforms that were made (since few states made major changes). Automobile insurance profits also rose substantially (NAIC 1994), thereby reducing the likelihood that firms would withdraw coverage. Not surprisingly, automobile insurance reform tended to diminish in importance as a policy agenda item. Certainly this issue is likely to reappear on the agenda at such time as there is another period of sharply rising rates. Until then, however, we would not expect much change in how politicians diagnose the automobile insurance problem; they are simply too busy paying attention to other issues.

An emphasis on stories also has some normative implications for the evaluation of decision making. As I stress in chapter 3, stories are not all created equal. Independent evidence can be brought to bear on stories' factual premises, and judgments can be made accordingly. In this regard, I contend that the Pogo Story was much better supported by the data than was the Profiteering Story. Hence we should take it as a positive sign when the Pogo Story replaced the Profiteering Story as the dominant one among decision makers. It may be that in other policy areas political scientists can not only identify which stories are dominant, but reach reasonable conclusions about which ones are more or less supportable. This will often be hard, and sometimes controversial. But I think it is worth attempting.

My research also solidifies the notion that institutional differences influence the ability to impose losses on powerful groups. However, it is important to be more precise about the extent to which the automobile insurance reform findings can be generalized to other policy areas. Two limitations on such generalization seem especially compelling. The first is that differences between the American and Canadian governmental systems appear most relevant to policy changes that require legislative action (such as adopting a no-fault system) and cannot be accomplished by executive action alone. Factors such as the multiple veto points in the American system might well be inconsequential in the latter situation. Additionally, it seems reasonable to surmise that the advantages of the parliamentary system for loss imposition are more pronounced when the defeat is borne by a relatively small group (e.g., lawyers, insurance companies) to advance the salient interests of the larger public. As has been stressed throughout this book, automobile insurance is an issue that can engage the broad middle class citizenry. Elected officials may be more willing to "take the flak" under such circumstances than they would be if the losers were a broad spectrum of voters, such as adult pensioners.[1]

This study also reinforces the methodological value of continuing to explore comparative policy development in the American states and Canadian provinces. In effect, a massive natural political experiment has occurred in North America: two long-time, federalist democracies with relatively similar political cultures (by world standards, if not in the opinion of many Canadians!), and similar levels of economic development, have operated under sharply different institutional arrangements. Yet political scientists have taken little advantage of this fact, especially with regard to comparing and contrasting the actions of subnational governments.[2] More work of this kind clearly is needed.

CONCLUSION

In examining decisions on issues such as automobile insurance reform, it is easy to become preoccupied with the clash of interests and miss a fundamental point about what guides politicians. Elected officials tend to want to solve problems that concern their constituents. Politicians are often unsure about how to do so, or hold different opinions about what will work. In such circumstances, politics is not easily reducible to the "bargaining game" that has commonly dominated depictions of how decisions are made, especially in the legislative arena.[3] Instead, politics is in large part a battle for the minds of elected officials.

As a discipline, political science in recent years has made a move toward emphasizing the importance of how the "politics of ideas" affects public policy choices. I applaud that move, but think we need to go further. More analysis of the stories that may underlie politicians' judgments would seem a promising place to start.

NOTES TO CHAPTER 8

1. On this point, see also Pierson and Weaver (1993, 114–15, note 5). By contrast, Rabe (1994, 24) argues that "in practice" it is not clear that the Canadian parliamentary system affords any advantages to imposing the losses necessitated by hazardous waste siting. However, the *benefits* from hazardous waste siting are not only widely distributed but unlikely to be salient to the larger public (i.e., those not adversely affected by the siting) in the way that reducing the costs of automobile insurance can be.

2. For an exception, see Rabe 1994. Rabe himself (1994, 22) notes the general lack of attention to comparative subnational policy making in the two countries.

3. On the dominance of bargaining models over more deliberative conceptions of legislative decision making, see especially Bessette 1994, ch. 3.

Appendix

Notes on Data Sources

The arguments in this book draw from a wide variety of data sources. While these sources are cited, some readers may find it helpful to refer to a single place for an overview of the information I used. This appendix provides such an overview.

AGGREGATE DATA

I rely heavily on previously published information about rates, costs of doing business, industry finances, characteristics of insurance systems, and other data relevant to automobile insurance in both the United States and Canada. The best source of information about automobile insurance in the American states is the National Association of Insurance Commissioners (NAIC), which produces a variety of helpful publications (e.g., the "Auto Insurance Database Report"). The Insurance Bureau of Canada (IBC) also publishes helpful industry statistics, but there are two problems with the IBC data: (1) the information is less thorough and less well processed than that collected by NAIC; and (2) the IBC information generally does not cover the four provinces with public automobile insurance systems (i.e., British Columbia, Manitoba, Quebec, and Saskatchewan). Information about these provinces can be obtained directly from the public corporations responsible for insurance provision; I mainly used reports from the Manitoba Public Insurance Corporation (MPIC).

An excellent source for information about the status of tort and no-fault laws in the states and provinces is Robert H. Joost, *Automobile Insurance and No-Fault Law 2d* (Deerfield, ILL: Clark, Boardman Callaghan, 1992), with supplements. This book summarizes current laws in each jurisdiction. It also provides an overview of recent statutory changes, as well as background data on such topics as the portion of automobile claimants represented by attorneys. To understand what reforms had been attempted in specific jurisdictions, and what reforms actually had been adopted, I drew mainly from the Joost book and the written survey described below.

SURVEYS

I made extensive use of two 1995 surveys. The first I conducted myself and was aimed at people familiar with policy making in the area of automobile insurance reform. The substantive focus was recent reform legislation. All subnational jurisdictions in Canada and the United States were included in the survey, except those in which more intensive case studies were conducted. In the United States, I mailed surveys to state insurance commissioners and state legislative staff listed in the latest National Conference of State Legislatures' *Legislative Staff Directory* as having expertise in insurance. In Canada, I mailed surveys to provincial insurance superintendents (some of whom forwarded letters to public insurance corporations) and regional offices of the IBC. I received one or more responses from people with information about all ten Canadian provinces, and all except five American states. I used the information from this survey especially in my analysis of the nature of the perceived public policy problem (see chapter 3) and the impact of government institutional differences (see chapter 7).

The second survey I conducted with Michael R. Powers, chairman of the Department of Risk, Insurance, and Healthcare Management at Temple University. This survey was directed at members of the American Risk and Insurance Association (ARIA) and American Economics Association (AEA) and was aimed at assessing the extent to which consensus about automobile insurance reform existed within the insurance "public policy community." (The survey of AEA members served to provide a comparison group.) A total of 363 usable questionnaires were obtained from this survey. In chapter 3 I draw upon this data for my arguments about the views of the expert community. Our findings are more extensively summarized in Lascher and Powers (1997). Anyone who wants to obtain a codebook and the raw data from this study should contact me.

CASE STUDIES

In general, my strategy for each of the case study jurisdictions was to rely on the following sources: (1) interviews (generally in person) with politicians, regulatory agency personnel, interest group representatives, newspaper reporters, academics, and others involved in policy making in the area of automobile insurance; (2) review of stories in the "newspaper(s) of record" in the jurisdiction (i.e., the *Philadelphia Inquirer*, the *Providence Journal-Bulletin*, the *Globe and Mail* [Toronto], and the *Toronto Star*); (3) and review of written material prepared by interested parties in the insurance reform controversies (e.g., regulatory agencies, public

Case Studies

insurance corporations, trial attorneys, insurance companies). Although only some people I interviewed requested anonymity, for this book I opted to treat all contacts as anonymous, except in a few cases when I specifically did not offer anonymity *and* I believed the identity of the interviewee was especially important to my argument (notably, this applies to my interview with then Governor Robert P. Casey of Pennsylvania).

There were some differences in my approach in each of the three jurisdictions. My data collection effort in Rhode Island was undertaken as the decision on the 1993 legislation was unfolding. I conducted the most interviews in that state, meeting with more than twenty-five lawmakers and a wide variety of other people. The physical proximity of the state to where I was living at the time allowed for repeated visits. I also was motivated to conduct an especially large number of interviews because I began the Rhode Island case study with only a cursory understanding of the policy issue. Additionally, I witnessed some of the committee and floor action on reform legislation; for other such action I reviewed videotape prepared by the Rhode Island General Assembly Radio-TV Office. My case studies of events in Pennsylvania and Ontario were conducted "after the fact," and involved fewer interviews. In 1994 I made two visits to Harrisburg (the Pennsylvania state capital), one to Philadelphia, and one to Toronto (the Ontario provincial capital). Additionally, I interviewed by telephone some people involved in the Ontario insurance battles and for Pennsylvania I reviewed the verbatim transcripts of state legislative floor proceedings contained in the *Legislative Journal*. Again, it also should be noted that many features of the Ontario automobile insurance controversy had been well summarized in previous case studies conducted by others.

My approach to the three "mini-case study" jurisdictions (Manitoba, Saskatchewan, and Hawaii) generally mirrored that conducted in the larger case studies, except that I only conducted a handful of interviews and made a less thorough effort to collect relevant information from interested parties. I conducted telephone interviews with government officials and others knowledgeable about the insurance reform battles in Manitoba and Saskatchewan and reviewed newspaper articles from the *Winnipeg Free Press* (available in microfilm form at the Harvard University library), and the *Leader-Post Regina* (clippings were sent to me by a reporter). I also was provided three documents that were especially helpful: 1) a binder of material from MPIC including, among other things, the statutory language for the no-fault act, summaries of the effects of the new law, and the 1993 MPIC discussion paper addressing pure no-fault and other policy options; 2) the two-volume 1988 "Kopstein Commission" report on automobile insurance in Manitoba; and 3) the 1993 consultant's report recommending adoption of a pure no-fault plan in Saskatchewan. My research assistant, Matthew Newman, made one visit to Hawaii in the summer of 1995 and interviewed a variety of people at that time. He also collected newspaper clippings from the two Honolulu papers (the *Honolulu Star-Bulletin* and *Honolulu Advertiser*) and other information.

References

All-Industry Research Advisory Council (AIRAC). 1988. "Attorney Involvement in Auto Injury Claims." Oak Brook, IL: AIRAC.

Arnold, R. Douglas. 1990. *The Logic of Congressional Action*. New Haven: Yale University Press.

Atkinson, Michael M., and Robert A. Nigol. 1989. "Selecting Policy Instruments: Neo-Institutional and Rational Choice Interpretations of Automobile Insurance in Ontario." *Canadian Journal of Political Science* 22: 107–35.

Baetz, Mark C. 1993. "Automobile Insurance in Ontario." Case Study Number G-92-130-01, The Laurier Institute for Business and Economic Studies, Wilfred Laurier University.

Barnes, Angela. 1988. "35%–40% Jump in Car Insurance Urged by Report." *Globe and Mail* [Toronto]. 6 December: A1, A2.

Berte, Marjorie M. 1991. *Hit Me—I Need the Money! The Politics of Auto Insurance Reform*. San Francisco: Institute for Contemporary Studies.

Bessette, Joseph A. 1994. *The Mild Voice of Reason: Deliberative Democracy and American Government*. Chicago: University of Chicago Press.

Bianco, William T. 1994. *Trust: Representatives and Constituents*. Ann Arbor: University of Michigan Press.

Bilinkoff, Arlene. 1993. "Tories' MPIC Switcheroo." *Winnipeg Free Press*. 18 May: A6.

Blau, Lauren. 1993. "Proposition 103 Turns 5; So Does Court Fight." *Los Angeles Daily Journal*. 106: 3.

Botticelli, Ann. 1995. "How End to No-Fault May Save You Money." *Honolulu Advertiser*. 8 February: A1, A7.

Brett, George. 1989a. "Insurers Incredulous at Limit." *Toronto Star*. 18 April: A1, A21.

———. 1989b. "Insurers Back, Lawyers Oppose Plan to Reform Auto Insurance." *Toronto Star*. 16 September: C3.

Cain, Bruce, and Nathaniel Persily. 1995. "Creating an Accountable Legislature: The Parliamentary Option for California Government," in *Constitutional Reform in California*, eds. Cain and Roger Noll, 163–93. Berkeley: Institute of Governmental Studies Press.

California Journal. 1996. "March 1996 Primary Ballot Propositions." 27: 36–38, 41–47.

Canadian Parliamentary Guide. 1989. Toronto: Globe and Mail Publishing Company.

Carroll, Stephen J., James S. Kakalik, Nicholas M. Pace, and John L. Adams. 1991. *No-Fault Approaches to Compensating People Injured in Automobile Accidents.* Santa Monica, CA: RAND.
Cheit, Ross E., and Jonathan D. Youngwood. 1991. "How Not to Reform Auto Insurance." *Public Interest* (Summer): 67–79.
Citrin, Jack, and Donald P. Green. 1990. "The Self-Interest Motive in American Politics." *Research in Micropolitics* 3: 1–28.
Cohn, Gary, and Larry Fish. 1989. "Their Car Insurance Comes Cheap." *Philadelphia Inquirer,* 7 December: 1-A, 16-A, 17-A.
———, and Jodi Enda. 1989. "How Interest Groups Mold Pa.'s Auto Insurance System." *Philadelphia Inquirer,* 23 October: 1-A, 6-A.
Commonwealth of Pennsylvania. 1989a. *Legislative Journal.* House of Representatives. 13 June.
———. 1989b. *Legislative Journal.* House of Representatives. 12 December.
———. 1990. *Legislative Journal.* House of Representatives. 7 February.
Crotty, Patricia McGee. 1993. "Pennsylvania: Individualism Writ Large." In *Interest Group Politics in the Northeastern States,* eds. Ronald J. Hrebenar and Clive S. Thomas. University Park, PA: Pennsylvania State University Press.
Cummins, J. David, and Sharon Tennyson. 1992. "Controlling Automobile Insurance Costs." *Journal of Economic Perspectives* 6: 95–115.
Cummins, J. David, and Mary A. Weiss. 1992a. "Incentive Effects of No-Fault Automobile Insurance: Evidence from Insurance Claim Data." In *Contributions to Insurance Economics,* ed. Georges Dionne. Boston: Kluwer Academic Publishers.
———. 1992b. "Regulation and the Automobile Insurance Crisis." *Regulation* 15: 48–59.
D'Arcy, Stephen P. 1982. "An Economic Theory of Insurance Regulation." Ph.D. dissertation, University of Illinois.
———. 1985. "The Perceived Restrictiveness of Property-Liability Insurance Laws." *Journal of Insurance Regulation* 3: 307–14.
Daysog, Rick. 1995. "Auto Insurance: How Much Reform Will Work Best?" *Honolulu Star-Bulletin.* 31 January: A–1, A–6.
Derthick, Martha, and Paul J. Quirk. 1985. *The Politics of Deregulation.* Washington, DC: The Brookings Institution.
Devlin, Rose Anne. 1992. "Liability Versus No-Fault Automobile Insurance Regimes: An Analysis of the Experience in Quebec." In *Contributions to Insurance Economics,* ed. Georges Dionne. Boston: Kluwer Academic Publishers.
———. 1993. "Automobile Insurance in Ontario: Public Policy and Private Interests." *Canadian Public Policy* 19: 298–310.
Dodson, James. 1993. "The Battle for the Soul of Rhode Island." *Yankee* 57: 76–88, 118–31.
Doukas, Ozzie, ed. 1989. *The Pennsylvania Manual, Volume 109.* Harrisburg: Commonwealth of Pennsylvania.
Duggan, John F. 1994. "The Use and Abuse of Peer Review Organizations in Pennsylvania: An Analysis of the Private Enterprise Peer Review System under the Motor Vehicle Financial Responsibility Law of 1990." *Dickinson Law Review.* 98: 463–83.

References

Dyer, James A. 1976. "Do Lawyers Vote Differently? A Study of Voting on No-Fault Insurance." *Journal of Politics* 38: 452–56.

Ehrenhalt, Alan. 1991. *The United States of Ambition: Politicians, Power and the Pursuit of Office.* New York: Random House.

Enda, Jodi. 1989a. "Senate Panel Ignores House Auto-Rate Bills." *Philadelphia Inquirer.* 22 June: 1–A

———. 1989b. "Casey Attacks GOP Insurance Plan." *Philadelphia Inquirer.* 27 June: 5–B.

———. 1989c. "Senate Kills Casey Auto Plan." *Philadelphia Inquirer.* 29 June: 1–A, 21–A.

———. 1989d. "2 Auto Bills Are Passed." *Philadelphia Inquirer.* 30 June: 1–A, 4–A.

———. 1989e. "Why Casey's Auto-Insurance Plan Collapsed in Senate." *Philadelphia Inquirer.* 2 July: 1–F, 6–F.

———. 1989f. "Insurance Bill Backed by Panel." *Philadelphia Inquirer.* 6 December: 1–B.

———. 1989g. "Senate Balks at Casey's Auto Plan." *Philadelphia Inquirer.* 12 December: 1–A, 14–A.

———. 1989h. "State House Rejects Car Insurance Plan." *Philadelphia Inquirer,* 13 December: 1–A, 6–A.

———. 1989i. "Wild Week Ends with Some Hope for Insurance Bill." *Philadelphia Inquirer.* 17 December: 1–E, 4–E.

England, Catherine. 1994. "Redlining by the Numbers." *American Enterprise* 5: 12–16.

Feldthusen, Bruce. 1990. "Prices and Politics: Automobile Insurance Rate Regulation in Ontario." *Canadian Insurance Law Review* 1: 283–309.

Fenno, Richard F., Jr. 1973. *Congressmen in Committees.* Boston: Little, Brown and Company.

———. 1978. *Home Style: Representatives in Their Districts.* Boston: Little, Brown and Company.

Ferguson, Derek. 1990. "Province's Auto Plan Due in Spring," *Toronto Star.* 21 November: A8.

Fiorina, Morris P. 1992. *Divided Government.* New York: MacMillan.

Fish, Larry, and Gary Cohn. 1989. "Why Phila. Car Insurance is Nation's Highest." *Philadelphia Inquirer.* 22 October: 1–A, 18–A, 19–A.

Fleming, Robert J., and J. E. Glenn, eds. 1997. *Fleming's Canadian Legislatures 1997.* Toronto: University of Toronto Press.

Globe and Mail [Toronto]. 1989 "50,000 Protest Insurance Plan." 4 January: A3.

Gooderham, Mary. 1988. "Didn't Say Insurance Ceiling Was Forever, Peterson Insists." *Globe and Mail* [Toronto]. 7 December: A1, A2.

Gorham, Bradford. 1993. "Finding Fault with Some No-Faulters." *Providence Journal-Bulletin.* 24 May: A14.

Gurwitt, Rob. 1994. "Reform in the Most Unlikely Places." *Governing* 7: 36–41.

Harley, Kevin. 1989. "The Auto Insurance Debate: Competition and Consumer Choice." Harrisburg, PA: The Commonwealth Foundation for Public Policy Alternatives.

Harrington, Scott E. 1993. "Rate Suppression." *Journal of Risk and Insurance* 59: 185–201.

———. 1994. "State Decisions to Limit Tort Liability: An Empirical Analysis of No-Fault Automobile Insurance Laws." *Journal of Risk and Insurance* 61: 276–94.
Honolulu Advertiser. 1995. " 'No Sue' Version of No-Fault Outlined." 15 February: A3.
Impact Communications. 1993. *Decision Makers 1993–94*. Providence: Impact Communications.
Insurance Bureau of Canada. 1994. *Facts of the General Insurance Industry in Canada*. Toronto: Insurance Bureau of Canada.
Insurance Information Institute. 1993. *The Fact Book 1993: Property/Casualty Insurance Facts*. New York: Insurance Information Institute.
Joost, Robert H. 1992. *Automobile Insurance and No-Fault Law 2d*. Deerfield, ILL: Clark, Boardman Callaghan.
Keeton, Robert E., and Jeffrey O'Connell. 1965. *Basic Protection for the Traffic Victim: A Blueprint for Reforming Automobile Insurance*. Boston: Little, Brown and Company.
Kelman, Steven. 1987. *Making Public Policy: A Hopeful View of American Government*. New York: Basic Books.
Kennedy, David M. 1987. "California Welfare Reform." Case study C16–87–782.0, Kennedy School of Government, Harvard University.
King, Gary, Robert O. Keohane, and Sidney Verba. 1994. *Designing Social Inquiry: Scientific Inference in Qualitative Research*. Princeton: Princeton University Press.
Kingdon, John W. 1989. *Congressmen's Voting Decisions*, 3rd. ed. Ann Arbor: University of Michigan Press.
———. 1995. *Agendas, Alternatives, and Public Policies*, 2d ed. New York: HarperCollins.
Kopstein, Robert L. 1988. *Report of the Autopac Review Commission*. Winnipeg: Government of Manitoba.
Krehbiel, Keith. 1991. *Information and Legislative Organization*. Ann Arbor: University of Michigan Press.
Lakoff, George. 1996. *Moral Politics: What Conservatives Know That Liberals Don't*. Chicago: University of Chicago Press.
Lascher, Edward L., Jr. 1996. "Assessing Legislative Deliberation: A Preface to Empirical Analysis." *Legislative Studies Quarterly* 21: 501–19.
———. 1998. "Loss Imposition and Institutional Characteristics: Learning from Automobile Insurance Reform in North America." *Canadian Journal of Political Science* 31: 143–64.
———, Steven Kelman, and Thomas J. Kane. 1993. "Policy Views, Constituency Pressure, and Congressional Action on Flag Burning." *Public Choice* 76: 79–102.
———, and Michael R. Powers. 1997. "Expert Opinion and Automobile Insurance Reform: An Empirical Assessment." *Journal of Insurance Regulation* 16: 197–222.
Laskow, Paul. 1990. "The New Insurance Law Is a Loser." *Philadelphia Inquirer*. 14 February: 11–A.
Legislative Analyst, State of California. 1990. "Proposition 103—One Year

References

Later," in *1990–91 Budget: Perspectives and Issues*. Sacramento: Legislative Analyst's Office.

Legislative Budget and Finance Committee, Pennsylvania General Assembly. 1993. "Evaluation of the Medical Cost Containment Provisions of Act 1990-6." Harrisburg, PA.

Litzenberger, Robert H., and Blaine F. Nye. 1987. "Level of Competition in the California Private Passenger Automobile Insurance Market." Sacramento: Association of California Insurance Companies.

Lupia, Arthur. 1994. "Shortcuts Versus Encyclopedias: Information and Voting Behavior in California Insurance Reform Elections." *American Political Science Review* 88: 63–76.

Macey, Jonathan R., and Geoffrey P. Miller. 1993. *Costly Policies: State Regulation and Antitrust Exemption in Insurance Markets*. Washington: AEI Press.

MacKay, Scott, and G. Wayne Miller. 1992. "Assembly Incumbents Fare Well; GOP Makes Slight Gains." *Providence Journal-Bulletin*. 4 November: A3.

Mackie, Richard. 1990. "Elston Attacks Disgruntled Lawyers over Auto Insurance Plan." *Globe and Mail* [Toronto]. 9 January: A3.

MacLeod, Robert. 1989. "No-Fault Insurance Planned in Ontario." *Globe and Mail* [Toronto]. 16 September: A1, A2.

Mandryk, Murray. 1994a. "Bergman Wants Debate on Insurance." *Leader-Post Regina*. 5 May: B10.

———. 1994b. "Egads! The Lawyers Right?" *Leader-Post Regina*. 6 May: A4.

Manitoba Bar Association (MBA). 1989. "An Evaluation of the Autopac Review Commission Recommendation That a Total No Fault Automobile Insurance Scheme Be Implemented in Manitoba." MBA.

Manitoba Public Insurance Corporation (MPIC). 1993. "Review of Alternate Personal Injury Plans." Winnipeg: MPIC.

Marmor, Theodore R. 1993. "Health Care Reform in the United States: Patterns of Fact and Fiction in the Use of Canadian Experience." *American Review of Canadian Studies* 23: 47–64.

Mayhew, David R. 1991. *Divided We Govern: Party Control, Lawmaking, and Investigations, 1946–1990*. New Haven: Yale University Press.

Meier, Kenneth J. 1988. *The Political Economy of Regulation: The Case of Insurance*. New York: State University of New York Press.

Miller, Dan. 1998. "Auto Choice: Impact on Cities and the Poor." Joint Economic Committee Study, United States Congress.

Miller, Mark C. 1995. *The High Priests of American Politics: The Role of Lawyers in American Political Institutions*. Knoxville. University of Tennessee Press.

Mitchell, Bob. 1989. "Lawyers Vow to Fight No-Fault Insurance Bid." *Toronto Star*. 19 September: A4.

Moncrief, Gary. 1990. "Contrasting the American and Canadian Subnational Legislatures." *Canadian Parliamentary Review* (Autumn): 5–17.

———. 1994. "Professionalization and Careerism in Canadian Provincial Assemblies: Comparison to U.S. State Legislatures." *Legislative Studies Quarterly* 19: 33–47.

Monahan, Patrick. 1995. *Storming the Pink Palace: The NDP in Power: A Cautionary Tale*. Toronto: Lester Publishing.

Mooney, Christopher Z. 1994. "Measuring U.S. State Legislative Professionalism: An Evaluation of Five Indices." *State and Local Government Review* 26: 70–78.
Motley, Wanda. 1993. "Auto Insurers Seeking Rate Decreases in Pa." *Philadelphia Inquirer.* 21 July: B1, B2.
Mucciaroni, Gary. 1992. "The Garbage Can Model and the Study of Policy Making: Critique." *Polity* 24: 459–82.
———. 1995. *Reversals of Fortune: Public Policy and Private Interests.* Washington, DC: The Brookings Institution.
Muir, William K., Jr. 1982. *Legislature: California's School for Politics.* Chicago: University of Chicago Press.
National Association of Insurance Commissioners (NAIC). 1993. "Auto Insurance Database Report." Kansas City: NAIC.
———. 1994. "Report on Profitability by Line by State 1993." Kansas City: NAIC.
O'Connell, Jeffrey. 1989. "No-Fault Insurance: Back by Popular (Market) Demand?" *San Diego Law Review* 26: 993–1015.
O'Donnell, Allan. 1991. *Automobile Insurance in Ontario.* Toronto: Butterworths.
Ohio Casualty Insurance v. Insurance Department of the Commonwealth of Pennsylvania, 584 Atlantic 2d 1160 (Commonwealth of Pennsylvania 1991).
Osborne, Coulter A. 1988. *Report of Inquiry into Motor Vehicle Accident Compensation in Ontario.* Toronto: Ontario Ministry of the Attorney General and the Ministry of Financial Institutions.
Peltzman, Sam. 1976. "Toward a More General Theory of Regulation." *Journal of Law and Economics,* 19: 276–94.
Pennington, Nancy, and Reid Hastie. 1993a. "The Story Model for Juror Decision Making." In *Inside the Juror,* ed. Hastie. Cambridge: Cambridge University Press.
———. 1993b. "Reasoning in Explanation-Based Decision Making." *Cognition* 49 (1993): 123–63.
Philadelphia Inquirer. 1989a. "Hitting the Brakes." 16 June: 22–A.
———. 1989b. "Auto Insurance Clash: The Forces of Evil Confront the Forces of Good in the Pa. Senate Today—Who Will Win?" 11 December: 14–A.
———. 1990. "Now They Tell Us." 18 April: 10–A.
Pierson, Paul D., and R. Kent Weaver. 1993. "Imposing Losses in Pension Policy." In *Do Institutions Matter? Government Capabilities in the United States and Abroad,* ed. Weaver and Bert A. Rockman. Washington, DC: The Brookings Institution.
Powers, Michael R. 1989. "Automobile Insurance in Pennsylvania: Problems and Solutions." Harrisburg: Pennsylvania Insurance Department.
Providence Journal-Bulletin. 1993. "Their Fault." 14 May: A14.
Quirk, Paul J. 1990. "Deregulation and the Politics of Ideas in Congress." In *Beyond Self-Interest,* ed. Jane J. Mansbridge. Chicago: University of Chicago Press.
———, and Gary Mucciaroni. 1996. "Does Deliberation Really Matter? Models of Information in Policymaking." Presented at the Annual Meeting of the American Political Science Association, San Francisco.

References

Rabe, Barry G. 1994. *Beyond NIMBY: Hazardous Waste Siting in the United States and Canada*. Washington, DC: The Brookings Institution.

Riggs, Doug. 1993. "State of Disgrace." *Providence Sunday Journal*. 7 January: 6–16.

Rosenthal, Alan. 1993. *The Third House: Lobbyists and Lobbying in the States*. Washington, DC: CQ Press.

———. 1998. *The Decline of Representative Democracy: Process, Participation, and Power in State Legislatures.* Washington, DC: CQ Press.

Smith, Eric, and Randall Wright. 1992. "Why Is Automobile Insurance in Philadelphia So Damn Expensive?" *American Economic Review* 82: 756–72.

Smith, Steven K., Carol J. DeFrances, Patrick A. Langan, and John Goerdt. 1995. "Tort Cases in Large Counties." U.S. Department of Justice, Bureau of Justice Statistics (April).

Sniderman, Paul M., Joseph F. Fletcher, Peter H. Russell, and Philip E. Tetlock. 1996. *The Clash of Rights: Liberty, Equality, and Legitimacy in Pluralist Democracy*. New Haven: Yale University Press.

Sobeco Ernst & Young. 1993. "Saskatchewan Government Insurance: Automobile Injury Study." Sobeco Ernst & Young.

Spiro, Peter, and Daniel Mirvish. 1989. "Whose No-Fault Is It, Anyway?" *Washington Monthly* (October): 24–28.

Squire, Peverill. 1988. "Career Opportunities and Membership Stability in Legislatures." *Legislative Studies Quarterly* 13: 65–82.

———. 1992. "Legislative Professionalism and Membership Diversity in State Legislatures." *Legislative Studies Quarterly* 17: 69–79.

Standard & Poor's Corporation. 1988. *Industry Outlook on Property/Casualty Insurance*. New York: Standard & Poor's.

Stigler, George J. 1971. "The Theory of Economic Regulation." *Bell Journal of Economics and Management Science* 2: 3–21.

Story, Alan. 1989. "Car Rates Capped at 7.6%." *Toronto Star*. 18 April: A1.

Sullivan, Brian P. 1994. "Has Hawaii's Legislature Changed? Despite New Laws, Insurers Unsure." *Auto Insurance Report* 1 (28 March): 1, 4–8.

———. 1996. "State Farm Takes Up the Challenge; Calls Hawaii Rate Cut Reasonable." *Auto Insurance Report 1995 Yearbook*. Liguna Niguel, CA: Risk Communications.

Sutton, Brent. 1991. "The Property and Casualty Insurance Industry: Mid-Term Prospects and the Challenges Ahead." Ottawa: The Conference Board of Canada.

Thomas, Clive S. 1993. "The Changing Nature of Interest-Group Activity in the Northeast." In *Interest Group Politics in the Northeastern States*, ed. Ronald J. Hrebenar and Clive S. Thomas. University Park, PA: Pennsylvania State University Press.

Thompson's World Insurance News. 1996. "Spaghetti Junction: Ontario Tories Drive Auto Insurance Along a New Superhighway." 19 February.

Tillinghast (a Towers Perrin Company). 1993. "Analysis of Rhode Island Automobile Insurance System." Boston: Tillinghast.

Toronto Star. 1989. "Elston's Saw-Off on Car Insurance." 16 September: D2.

Turner, Janice. 1990. "Guru Nader Urges Ontario to Call Auto Insurers' Bluff." *Toronto Star*. 21 January: F8.

References

Walker, William. 1989a. "Rate Fiasco Could Make Public Auto Insurance Inevitable." *Toronto Star.* 18 April: A21.

———. 1989b. "How an Auto-Insurance Promise Hit the Ditch." *Toronto Star.* 2 July: B–1, B–4.

———. 1989c. "Michigan Bans Right to Sue for Most Pain and Suffering." *Toronto Star.* 3 July: A16.

Walkom, Thomas. 1989. "The $143 Million Insurance Subsidy." *Toronto Star.* 16 September: A9.

———. 1994. *Rae Days.* Toronto: Key Porter Books.

Weaver, R. Kent, and Bert A. Rockman, eds. 1993a. *Do Institutions Matter? Government Capabilities in the United States and Abroad.* Washington, DC: The Brookings Institution.

———. 1993b. "When and How Do Institutions Matter?" In *Do Institutions Matter?*, eds. Weaver and Rockman. Washington, DC: The Brookings Institution.

Weisberg, Herbert J., and Richard Derrig. 1992. "The System Misfired." *Best's Review* (December): 37–40, 87.

White, Graham. 1989. *The Ontario Legislature: A Political Analysis.* Toronto: University of Toronto Press.

———, and Gary Levy. 1989. "Introduction: The Comparative Analysis of Canadian Provincial and Territorial Legislative Assemblies." In *Provincial and Territorial Legislatures in Canada*, eds. White and Levy. Toronto: University of Toronto Press.

Whitehouse, Sheldon. 1993. Memo to Rhode Island Governor Bruce Sundlun, 22 January.

Wildavsky, Aaron. 1980. *How to Limit Government Spending.* Berkeley: University of California Press.

Winnipeg Free Press. 1993. "Risking No-Fault." 7 May: A6.

Wyatt, Mark. 1994. "No-Fault Auto Insurance Opposed." *Leader-Post Regina.* 26 February: A5.

Index

Act 6 (Pennsylvania), 52–55, 62, 65–71, 74, 90
  (*see also* Casey, Robert)
American culture versus Canadian culture, 8–9, 11 n.11, 124
American Economics Association, 128
American Risk and Insurance Association (ARIA), 14, 47–48, 51 nn. 12–14, 128
American states
  automobile insurance data and laws, 127–28
  common problem of automobile insurance rates in, 4, 120
  governments of, 7–8
  regulation of automobile insurance in, 6–7, 27–28
  requirement for purchase of automobile insurance in, 25–26
  (*see also* separation-of-powers system)
Arnold, R. Douglas, 16–18, 21, 23 n.4, 63, 82
Automobile Insurance Task Force (Rhode Island), 76

Beer, Samuel, 92
Berte, Marjorie, 24, 42
Bessette, Joseph 73 n.26
British Columbia, 27, 127
British House of Commons, 8, 92

California, 4–5, 7, 38–39, 58, 61, 65, 73 n.22, 77, 81
  Proposition 103 in, 38–39, 58, 73 n.22, 77, 81
Canadian culture. *See* American culture versus Canadian culture
Canadian provinces
  automobile insurance data and laws, 127–28
  common problem of insurance rates in 4, 120
  governments of, 7–8
  regulation of automobile insurance in, 6–7, 27–28
  requirement for purchase of automobile insurance, 25
  (*see also* Westminster parliamentary system)
capture theory, 13–14
Casey administration and Casey plan. *See* Casey, Robert
Casey, Robert, 5, 10, 52–53, 55–74, 81–87, 90, 101, 122, 129
causal stories, 2, 9, 20–23, 23 n.5, 24, 40–47, 63–64, 121–25
  (*see also* Pogo Story; Profiteering Story)
Cayetano, Benjamin, 114–15
Citrin, Jack, 29
Congress, U.S., 19, 27, 80
Congressional Record, 71 n.1
Connecticut, 79, 109

139

consumer groups and automobile insurance reform, 39
  (see also Nader, Ralph; Ocean State Action)
Cooperative Commonwealth Federation. See New Democratic Party
cues on the merits, 20, 22, 63
  (see also causal stories)
Cummings, Glen, 111–12
Cummins, J. David, 25–26, 41–42

D'Arcy, Stephen, 14, 23 n.3
deliberation, 1–2, 23 n.5, 87
  (see also causal stories; politics of ideas)
Democratic Party, 53, 75, 89 n.14, 114–15, 122
Dennenberg, Herb, 52
Department of Business Regulation (DBR), Rhode Island, 76–78, 86–87
  (see also Whitehouse, Sheldon)
Derthick, Martha, 19–20
District of Columbia, 10 n.3

Elston, Murray, 94–97
Evans, Leonard, 111–12, 118 n.7

Feldthusen, Bruce, 33, 100
Foster, Constance, 72 n.5
Freind, Stephen, 52, 56, 59, 72 nn.10, 19, 83, 122

Georgia, 109
Globe and Mail [Toronto], 128
Gorham, Bradford, 81, 83, 84, 88 n.10, 89 n.17
Green, Donald, 29

Harrington, Scott, 14–15, 22
Hastie, Reid, 21
Hawaii, 106, 111, 114–15, 118–19 n.15, 120, 129–30
Hayden, Richard, 56, 59, 60, 72 nn.5, 15, 83, 122
Herfindahl index of industry concentration, 50–51 n.12
Honolulu Advertiser, 130
Honolulu Star-Bulletin, 130

Illinois, 28
Insurance Bureau of Canada (IBC), 97–99, 102, 127–28
Insurance Federation of Pennsylvania (IFP), 57, 71, 73 n.25
Iowa, 33
Irons, William, 89 n.17

Joost, Robert, 127

Kansas, 33
Kelly, Paul, 77, 80–81, 83–84
Kelly, Walt, 50 n.9
Kennedy, Brian, 84
Kentucky, 110
Kingdon, John, 1, 21, 23, 24, 29, 36
Kopstein, Robert, and Kopstein Commission, 118 nn.5, 8, 10, 129
Kormos, Peter, 97–99, 104
Krehbiel, Keith, 12, 18–19

Lascher, Edward, 23 n.5, 47–48, 128
lawyer-legislators, 77–78, 82–85, 89, 107, 116, 117 n.2, 121, 123
Leader-Post Regina, 129

Index

Legislative Budget and Finance
 Committee (Pennsylvania), 66, 71
Legislative Journal (Pennsylvania),
 71 n.1, 129
Levy, Gary, 8
Liberal Party (Manitoba), 118 n.11
Liberal Party (Ontario), 5, 33,
 91–102, 104, 105 n.2, 107–08,
 117 n.2, 121–122
loss imposition, 10, 106–19, 122, 124

Macey, Jonathan, 27
Manitoba, 5, 7, 27, 34, 38–39, 45, 46,
 96, 106, 109, 111–13, 116–17, 120,
 127, 129–30
 automobile insurance reform in,
  5, 34, 39, 106, 109, 111–13, 116,
  120
 government of, 7
 public automobile insurance
  system in, 27, 38, 45, 96, 116–17,
  127
 sources of information for case
  study about, 129–30
Manitoba Public Insurance
 Corporation, 111–12, 118 nn.5, 8,
 127, 129
Massachusetts, 43
Mayhew, David, 108
McCarran-Ferguson Act, 27
Meier, Kenneth, 14, 23 n.2
Mercer Report (Ontario), 94–95
Michigan, 94, 102
Miller, Geoffrey, 27
Minnesota, 33–34
Missouri, 34
Monahan, Patrick, 104, 105 n.7
Mucciaroni, Gary, 23 nn.1, 6

Nader, Ralph, 9, 39, 41, 78–79, 87,
 98, 115

National Association of Insurance
 Commissioners (NAIC), 9, 35, 44,
 66, 127
National Conference of State
 Legislatures, 128
Nebraska, 7
New Democratic Party (NDP), 5,
 33, 37–38, 91–93, 96, 102–04,
 105 n.2, 111, 113–14, 117, 118 nn.11,
 12, 122
Newfoundland, 34
Newman, Matthew, 118–19 n.15, 130
New Jersey, 110
New York, 76, 78, 94, 102, 117
no-fault automobile insurance
 in American states versus
  Canadian provinces, 107–19
 consumer group views about, 38
 different types of systems, 37,
  43, 50 n.5, 72 n.9, 88 n.1,
  109–10
 essential features of, 36, 50 n.4
 in Hawaii, 114–15, 119 n.18
 incentives for driving behavior
  created by, 51 n.15, 71, 73 n.27
 losses necessitated by, 40, 44
 in Manitoba, 109, 111–13, 122
 as means of reforming
  automobile insurance, 4, 14–16,
  34, 36–38, 43, 49
 in Ontario, 90–105, 107–10,
  120–22
 in Pennsylvania, 52–73, 109–10,
  120, 122
 and Pogo Story, 43, 47
 and Profiteering story, 41, 45, 47
 as required coverage, 26
 in Rhode Island, 49–50 n.2, 74–89,
  107, 120–22
 in Saskatchewan, 109, 111–13,
  122
 separation-of-powers system
  versus Westminster

no-fault automobile, *continued*
  Parliamentary system and,
    107–19, 124
  sources of information about
    subnational laws regarding,
    127–28
  trial attorney views about, 38–39,
    50 n.8
Northwest Territories, 10 n.3
Nova Scotia, 7

Ocean State Action, 77–78, 81, 86–87,
  107
O'Connell, Jeffrey, 37
O'Donnell, Allan, 33, 102
Ohio, 34
Ontario, 5, 7, 9–10, 28, 32–33, 34, 38,
  47–49, 50 n.3, 72, 90–105, 106–09,
  113, 117, 120–21, 128–29
  automobile insurance reform in,
    5, 9–10, 32–33, 34, 38, 47–49, 50,
    72 n.14, 90–109, 113, 117, 120–21
  government and politics, 7,
    92–93, 104–05
  public automobile insurance
    system proposed for, 38, 91, 96,
    101–04
  regulation of automobile
    insurance in, 28, 50, 100
  sources of information for case
    study about, 128–29
Ontario Automobile Insurance
  Board (OAIB), 94–95, 97, 101–02
Ontario Motorist Protection Plan
  (OMPP), 96–99
Ontario Provincial Parliament. *See*
  Ontario, automobile insurance
  reform in; Ontario, government
  and politics
Osborne, Coulter and Osborne
  Report (Ontario), 96–97

parliamentary system. *See* Westminster parliamentary system
Pennington, Nancy, 21
Pennsylvania, 5, 9–10, 28, 32, 39,
  47–49, 52–73, 81–89, 91, 106,
  109–10, 120–22, 128–29
  automobile insurance reform in,
    5, 9–10, 32, 39, 47–49, 52–73, 91,
    106, 109–10, 120–22
  comparison to Rhode Island,
    81–89
  government and politics, 53,
    71 n.3, 89 n.15
  regulation of automobile
    insurance in, 28, 72 n.6
  sources of information for case
    study about, 128–29
Pennsylvania General Assembly. *See*
  Pennsylvania, automobile
  insurance reform in; Pennsylvania
  government and politics
Pennsylvania Insurance Department.
  See Casey, Robert
Pennsylvania Medical Society, 57
Pennsylvania Trial Lawyers
  Association (PTLA), 56–58, 60,
  73 n.20, 82
Peterson, David, 5, 93–95, 105 n.3
Philadelphia, rates problem in, 32,
  53–54, 57, 88
Philadelphia Inquirer, 56, 59, 64, 128
Pierson, Paul, 106
Pogo Story, 42–48, 50 n.10, 53, 63–64,
  86–87, 89 n.17, 91, 100–02, 121,
  124
policy community, insurance, 6, 9,
  47–48
  (*see also* American Risk and
    Insurance Association)
politics of ideas, 2, 12, 17–21, 23 n.5,
  63, 125
  (*see also* causal stories)
Powers, Michael, 47–48, 128

Index

pressure theory, 7, 12–17, 21–22, 23 n.1, 62–63, 81–86
Profiteering Story, 41–47, 63, 86–87, 89 n.17, 101, 103, 107, 121–22, 124
Progressive Conservative Party, 5, 91–93, 105 n.2, 111–13, 122
Providence Journal-Bulletin, 81, 128
public automobile insurance, 27, 38, 41, 45–46, 49, 96, 101–04, 116–17

Quebec, 27, 37, 94, 102, 112, 117, 127
Quirk, Paul, 19–20, 23 n.1, 74

Rabe, Barry, 119 n.22, 125 nn.1, 2
Rae, Bob, 103–04
RAND Corporation, 6
Republican Party, 53, 122
Rhode Island, 10, 31–32, 39, 47, 49–50 n.2, 62, 72 n.14, 74–89, 91, 98, 106–07, 116–17, 120–22, 128–29
  automobile insurance reform in, 10, 31–32, 39, 47, 49–50, 62, 72, 74–89, 91, 98, 106–07, 116–17, 120–22
  comparison to Pennsylvania, 81–89
  government and politics, 31, 75, 88 n.2, 89 nn.15, 16
  sources of information for case study about, 128–29
Rhode Island Ethics Commission, 78, 88
Rhode Island General Assembly. *See* Rhode Island, automobile insurance reform in; Rhode Island, government and politics
Rhode Island General Assembly Radio-TV Office, 88 n.5, 129
Rhode Island Trial Lawyers Association, 77

Rockman, Bert 2–3, 107–08, 113, 117 n.3

Saskatchewan, 27, 34, 38, 96, 106, 109, 111, 113–14, 127, 129–130
  automobile insurance reform in, 34, 106, 109, 111, 113–14
  public automobile insurance system in, 27, 38, 96, 116, 127
  sources of information for case study about, 129–30
Saskatchewan Trial Lawyers Association, 113
separation-of-powers system, 2–3, 7–8, 10, 11 n.10, 85, 106–19, 122, 124
Slater, David and Slater Report, 95
Squire, Peverill, 89 n.16
State Farm Insurance Company, 119 n.18
Stigler, George, 13, 23 n.2
stories. *See* causal stories
Sundlun, Bruce, 77, 85
Swart, Mel, 103

Tennyson, Sharon, 25–26, 41–42
Toronto Star, 98, 128
trial attorneys, and automobile insurance reform 38–39, 43, 50 n.8, 53, 59, 97, 99, 107, 112, 116, 120 (see also Pennsylvania Trial Lawyers Association, Rhode Island Trial Lawyers Association, Saskatchewan Trial Lawyers Association)

Utah, 34

Vermont, 34
Voter Revolt, 39

Walkom, Thomas, 103
Weaver, R. Kent, 2–3, 106–08, 113, 117 n.3
Westminster parliamentary system, 2–3, 8, 10, 11 n.10, 19, 91, 106–19, 122, 124–25
White, Graham, 8, 92, 104

Whitehouse, Sheldon, 76–77
 (*see also* Department of Business Regulation)
Winnipeg Free Press, 129
Wolfinger, Raymond, 11 n.7

Yukon, 10 n.3